D0512037

Whistleblowing at Work

WHISTLE BLOWING
at
Work

Edited by David B. Lewis

THE ATHLONE PRESS
LONDON & NEW BRUNSWICK, NJ

First published in 2001 by
THE ATHLONE PRESS
1 Park Drive, London NW11 7SG
and New Brunswick, New Jersey

British Library Cataloguing in Publication Data
*A catalogue record for this book is available
from the British Library*

ISBN   0 485 11561 1   HB
       0 485 12156 5   PB

Library of Congress Cataloging-in-Publication Data
*A catalog record for this book is available
from the Library of Congress*

Distributed in The United States, Canada and South America by
Transaction Publishers
390 Campus Drive
Somerset, New Jersey 08873

Typeset by Acorn Bookwork, Salisbury
Printed and bound in Great Britain by
Short Run Press Ltd, Exeter

Contents

Preface

In recent years, whistleblowing has caught the headlines. Properly so, many commentators think. Critical situations and disasters where the danger signals have been ignored or concealed have been brought to public attention and remedied. It is a salutary record, including the sinking of the *Herald of Free Enterprise*, the fire on the Piper Alpha oil rig, the Clapham rail crash and the infant heart surgery record at the Bristol Royal Infirmary. Sometimes the scandals are financial. We have to thank whistleblowers for bringing attention to the Bank of Credit and Commerce International and the European Commission itself. Whistleblowing has also played a vital part in exposing incidents of patient and child-care abuse and in the Arms to Iraq affair.

In the past, whistleblowers have acted at their peril, virtually unprotected by the law. But now the situation has been regularized. Following reports from the Nolan (now Neill) Committee on Standards in Public Life and three Private Members' Bills, the Public Interest Diclosure Act 1998 came into force in July 1999. This book examines the arguments for and against whistleblowing at work and explains the current legal framework. By drawing on the experience of contributors, it describes and analyses the significance of whistleblowing in different areas and offers legal, managerial, union and individual perspectives. Moreover, the book provides practical guidance on the implementation of whistleblowing policies and procedures.

David Lewis

List of Contributors

Tony Cutler, B.Sc. (Hons), is a Senior Lecturer in Management at Royal Holloway College, University of London. Previous publications include *Justice and Predictability* (with D. Nye) and *Managing the Welfare State* (with B. Waine).

Jennifer Frieze worked in a variety of community jobs as a researcher and teacher before joining UNISON as a Policy Officer. While working for the union she has written publications on a range of matters including: women's health, childcare, homecare services, local bargaining, nurses' pay and whistleblowing.

Stephen Homewood, B.A. (Hons), M.I. Arb, Barrister is a Principal Lecturer in Law and Chair of the Law Academic Group at Middlesex University. He teaches and researches in the areas of Environmental, Human Rights and Public Law and is a Council member of the UK Environmental Law Association.

Karen Jennings is currently Head of Nursing for UNISON. She practised as a registered nurse for 13 years, working in both hospitals and the community, before becoming a researcher in health and social policy. She has been responsible for a number of publications on older age, self-advocacy and the empowerment of health users and whistleblowing.

Chidi King is a barrister and former senior legal officer at Public Concern at Work. She joined Public Concern at Work in 1998, having spent 7 years in the voluntary sector advising and representing claimants in discrimination cases.

David Lewis, L.L.B. (Hons), M.A. (Industrial Relations), M.I.P.D., is Professor of Employment Law and Head of the Centre for Industrial and Commercial Law at Middlesex University. Previous publications include *Essentials of Employment Law* (with Malcolm Sargeant) and *Discipline* (with Phil James).

David Nye, B.A. (Hons), is a Senior Lecturer in Human Resource Management at Middlesex University. Recent articles (co-authored with Tony Cutler) relating to ethics, regulation and the tobacco industry have appeared in *International Journal of Health Services*, *European Journal of Public Health*, *Health Care Analysis*, and Health, Risk and Society.

Anne Ruff, L.L.B. (Hons), LL.M, P.G.C.E. (Tech), Barrister, is a Principal Lecturer in Law at Middlesex University. Previous publications include articles on education law in *Education and the Law*, *ACE Bulleting* and the *Solicitors Journal*. She is a contributing editor to the *Education Law Journal*.

Malcolm Sargeant, B.A. (Hons), Ph.D., is a Senior Lecturer in Law at Middlesex University. He also has extensive human resource management experience. Previous publications include *Essentials of Employment Law* (with David Lewis), *Maternity and Parental Rights* and *Age Discrimination in Employment*.

Kate Schroder, B.A. (Hons), is completing research into the issues surrounding whistleblowing and is undertaking commissioned research for Chichester District Council. She is a director of a company sourcing funding for community-based further and higher education projects and a regular speaker at conferences and seminars.

Peter Southwood, B.A. (Hons), M.B.A., Ph.D. (Peace Studies), is a Member of the Institute of Social and Ethical Accountability, a part-time lecturer at Middlesex University and a consultant on business ethics. Previous research includes two major surveys of human rights at the workplace.

Maureen Spencer, M.A., LL.M., Ph.D., is a Senior Lecturer in Law at Middlesex University. She has published in the fields of Evidence and Public Law.

Lucy Vickers, M.A. (Cantab), Ph.D., is a Senior Lecturer in Law at Oxford Brookes University. Her published work covers whistle-blowing, the Public Interest Disclosure Act and freedom of speech at work. She is currently preparing a book on *Freedom of Speech and Work*.

1

Introduction

DAVID LEWIS

This chapter looks at the problem of defining whistleblowing and asks whether whistleblowing is always in the public interest. It also suggests some whistleblower 'types' before summarising the contents of the chapters which follow.

WHAT IS WHISTLEBLOWING?

There is no universally accepted concept of whistleblowing. Some commentators define it narrowly as the reporting of illegal activities. Others prefer a more expansive definition which includes a broad range of wrongdoing. For example, in 1972 Ralph Nader defined whistleblowing as 'an act of a man or a woman who believing in the public interest overrides the interest of the organisation he serves,and publicly blows the whistle if the organisation is involved in corrupt, illegal, fraudulent or harmful activity'.[1]

More than twenty years later the Australian Senate Select Committee on Public Interest Whistleblowing adopted a more extensive definition: 'the whistleblower is a concerned citizen,totally or predominantly motivated by notions of public interest, who initiates of his or her own free will, an open disclosure about significant wrongdoing directly perceived in a particular occupational role, to a person or agency capable of investigagting the complaint and facilitating the correction of wrongdoing'.[2] Nevertheless, this Select Committee came to the commonsense conclusion that in the final analysis 'what is important is not the definition of the term, but the definition of the circumstances and conditions under which employees who disclose wrongdoing should be entitled to protection from retaliation'.[3] This is also the approach adopted in the United Kingdom by the Public Interest Disclosure Act 1998 (henceforward PIDA 1998). As will be seen in the next chapter, this legislation sets out: the types of disclosure which can give rise to protection ('qualifying disclosures'); the circumstances in which 'qualifying disclosures' will be protected ('protected disclosures'); and the categories of worker to whom the protection applies.

Although in some situations it may be difficult to decide whether a particular incident amounts to internal or external whistleblowing, there are good reasons for drawing a distinction.[4] Internal reporting offers advantages to both employer and worker. The employer is given the opportunity to deal with a problem without external pressures or publicity. From the worker's point of view, once a matter has been raised externally, they may be seen as an adversary and be more likely to suffer retaliation.[5] Thus workers who believe some wrongdoing is having an adverse effect on their terms and conditions of employment may choose to raise a grievance. Similarly, other internal channels may be available for specific matters, for example equal opportunities and health and safety procedures. However, if the subject of the concern does not fit within existing procedures and the matter is thought to be sufficiently serious, a worker may feel inclined to raise the matter externally.

It should also be noted that the law provides support for internal rather than external disclosures in two ways. First, while internal reporting to higher management might be perceived by supervisors as disloyal, it cannot be treated as a breach of the employee's common law duty of confidence or fidelity . Second, in determining whether there is a 'protected disclosure' within the meaning of PIDA 1998,regard will be had to whether the worker complied with a procedure authorized by the employer (see chapter 2).

IS WHISTLEBLOWING IN THE PUBLIC INTEREST?

A conventional but simplistic view of whistleblowers is that they are troublemakers who deserve to be punished for disloyalty.[6] An alternative approach is to treat them as dedicated individuals who provide a valuable safety net when other forms of regulation fail. Such an approach recognizes that workers are often in the best position to know whether there is malpractice within an organization. More positively, there is the 'enlightened self-interest approach' which sees whistleblowers as benefiting their employers by offering solutions to work problems. Those who first contact their managers about malpractice give them the chance to correct it before the matter escalates. It is not simply a question of internal communication being preferable to external whistleblowing; there is also the desirability of avoiding work stoppages over employee concerns. Thus whistleblowing can also be viewed as part of a strategy to maintain and improve quality. No doubt some employers would baulk at the idea of providing rewards for ethical behaviour. However, viewed from this 'quality' perspective, it may well be appropriate to offer financial incentives to those who disclose malpractice. Arguably, those who report concerns about malpractice are in an analogous position to those who propose improvements in organizational efficiency through a suggestion scheme. Indeed, both the USA and the UK governments provide financial inducements to 'blow the whistle' in certain circumstances.[7]

As regards the argument that whistleblowing poses a challenge to an organization's authority structure, this may not be the case where disclosures are positively encouraged and a channel for reporting is available (see chapter 5 for a discussion of the possible contents of whistleblowing procedures). If a mechanism for employees to raise their concerns is not provided, then either the problem will not be dealt with or the employee will feel obliged to air the matter externally.[8] As Lord Borrie put it: 'The result can be that conscientious and loyal employees become aggrieved or disillusioned.'[9]

Apart from helping to expose financial scandals, like those which occurred at BCCI, Barlow Clowes and with the Maxwell pensions, in some situations whistleblowing may be vital to preserve the health and safety of both the workforce and the general public. For example, the investigation into the *Herald of Free Enterprise* disaster in 1987 found that employees had aired their concerns on five previous occasions about the ship sailing with its bow doors open. A member of staff had even suggested fitting lights to the bridge to indicate whether the doors were closed. The inquiry concluded: 'If this sensible suggestion…had received the serious consideration it deserved this disaster might well have been prevented.'[10] The enquiry into the 1988 Piper Alpha oil platform disaster found that: 'workers did not want to put their continued employment in jeopardy through raising a safety issue that might embarrass management'.[11]

Thus, at one level, it can be argued that the disclosure of serious wrongdoing must always be in the public interest. However,it is important to acknowledge that there are circumstances in which this could be open to debate (see also chapter 3 on business ethics) – for example, if the disclosure leads to a factory shutdown and mass redundancies which decimate the local community. Equally, it should not be assumed that all whistleblowers are motivated by altruism. It is an unfortunate fact that concerns are sometimes raised out of malice. But does it necessarily follow that a malicious disclosure, perhaps of a serious crime, should not be regarded as being in the public interest? In chapter 2 we will see that current legislation is reluctant to accept that a person who makes a truthful disclosure in bad faith should be treated as acting in the public interest.

TYPES OF WHISTLEBLOWER

Dr Lucy Vickers draws a distinction between 'watchdog' and 'protest' whistleblowers.[12] The former discover and then expose wrongdoing in order to avoid safety or financial disasters. The latter raise more general concerns about the effects of their employer's activities. Both 'watchdog' and 'protest' whistleblowers would view themselves as good citizens, but there may be a suspicion that protest whistleblowing involves a political dimension. For this reason society may be more willing to encourage and protect those who speak out as 'watchdogs'. Put simply, it is more difficult to justify breaking a duty of confidence (see chapter 2) purely on the grounds of freedom of speech than where safety is compromised or fraud is suspected.

Although there may be certain characteristics which predispose a worker to report wrongdoing, existing research does not allow us to explain why one individual is prepared to 'blow the whistle' while others choose to turn a blind eye. A stereotypical approach is to regard whistleblowers as 'heroes' – loyal employees who report their concerns simply to ensure that institutional faults are rectified. Another view is that whistleblowers are 'idealists' who speak out because of the mismatch between their expectations and organizational realities. A third category is the 'defensive' whistleblower – the calculating employee who, in anticipation of disciplinary proceedings for poor performance, reports a concern with a view to establishing that the true reason for disciplinary action was victimization for speaking out. Finally, there is the 'vengeful' whistleblower – a former employee who reveals an employer's wrongdoing as a form of retribution for perceived mistreatment.[13]

How do we fit whistleblowers into these categories and is it necessary to do so? In practice, it may be virtually impossible to distinguish 'heroic' whistleblowers from those who have more selfish motives. Indeed, the decision to report a concern is likely to involve a complex mixture of factors which cannot be readily identified by either the whistleblower or an outsider. Perhaps for this reason the UK Parliament has chosen not to focus attention on motive other than to make employment protection rights dependent on workers demonstrating that they acted in good faith and not for personal gain (see chapter 2).

THE SCOPE OF THIS BOOK

The remainder of this book looks at whistleblowing from a variety of perspectives. In the next chapter, David Lewis and Maureen Spencer provide an overview of the law relating to whistleblowing in the UK.[14] They examine the ways in which laws have both constrained and encouraged the disclosure of information prior to the enactment of PIDA 1998. After a detailed discussion of the extent to which PIDA 1998 protects workers in defined circumstances, the authors briefly consider the position of whistleblowers in court proceedings. The chapter concludes with an evaluation of the current legal position and a comment on the potential impact of the Human Rights Act 1998.

In chapter 3, Tony Cutler and David Nye look at whistleblowing from a business ethics perspective. They compare the 'stakeholder' and the 'shareholder agent' (or 'classical') approaches to corporate social responsibility and outline their implications for whistleblowing. Having applied these approaches to two business scenarios, the authors then re-examine the 'classical' view in order to produce a more sophisticated interpretation. This refined 'classical' view is then used to analyse the business settings described earlier and different conclusions are drawn to those previously suggested. The chapter concludes by locating the various approaches to corporate social responsibility in wider ethical frameworks and by considering their implications for the debate about whether or not there is a duty to 'blow the whistle'.

Chapter 4 offers practising and trainee accountants a practical guide to help them decide under what circumstances it may be justified to 'blow the whistle' on firms or colleagues where malpractice is suspected. Peter Southwood believes that whistleblowing must be placed in the broader context of accounting ethics, although the profession itself tends to define ethics quite narrowly. Consequently, the main ethical theories are briefly reviewed, together with the relevant provisions of the codes of conduct adopted by the professional bodies, in order to examine the problems accountants face when performing their duties. Case studies are used to illustrate the ethical dilemmas of whistleblowing and how far the broad or narrow definitions of accounting ethics may assist. The author reveals an uneasy tension between the need for professionals to abide by a Code of Ethics (and thus respect client confidentiality) and recognition of a wider obligation to society which may, exceptionally, necessitate whistleblowing.

In chapter 5, David Lewis and Malcolm Sargeant look at whistleblowing from a human resource management perspective. They explain why employers should have a whistleblowing policy, discuss who should be involved in formulating such a policy and outline its possible contents. Having identified who and what should be covered by a procedure, the authors confront a range of practical issues. For example, the problems of confidentiality and anonymity are addressed as well as the difficulties of dealing with reprisals and malicious allegations. The authors point to the need for potential whistleblowers to have access to advice and assistance and then consider with whom and how a concern might be raised. They also suggest how employers should handle concerns and recommend that whistleblowing procedures are both effectively communicated and monitored. The authors conclude that such procedures can help to contribute towards an ethical and efficient image of the organization as well as minimizing the possibility of falling foul of the law.

Chapter 6 looks at the particular duties and provisions that apply to potential whistleblowers who work in the National Health Service (henceforward NHS). The special duty of patient confidentiality is examined together with its impact on the extent to which staff can 'blow the whistle'. This includes a consideration of the professional codes of conduct for nursing and medical staff and a discussion of their impact on the scope of the duty of confidence and the need to protect the public interest. Lucy Vickers then assesses recent policy initiatives, such as the recommendations of the Nolan Committee, the NHS Executive's Guidance for Staff on Relations with the Public and the Media, ministerial statements on freedom of speech in the NHS and updates to the NHS Executive's Guidance in the light of PIDA 1998. Finally, the application of PIDA 1998 to the NHS is examined.

In chapter 7, Stephen Homewood scrutinizes the role and methods of encouraging whistleblowing in local government. Having outlined the current structure and functions of local government, the specific mechanisms for providing scrutiny and accountability are discussed. The author then considers the recommendations of the Nolan Committee and the impact of Codes of Conduct for both local government officers and elected councillors. Recent and proposed legislation affecting the structure, constitution and organization of local government is also examined and an assessment is made of the potential impact of both the Human Rights Act 1998 and the Freedom of Information Bill. The author concludes that this range of recent developments may have more of an impact on standards in local government than PIDA 1998 itself.

Chapter 8 looks at how schools, colleges and universities might cope with disclosures in the public interest. Anne Ruff and David Lewis identify specific issues which may give rise to whistleblowing in education. These include: concerns about the competence of colleagues; health and safety issues; and allegations of fraud or other misconduct, including sexual abuse. The authors look briefly at the requirements of and procedures available under current education legislation and assess the impact of PIDA 1998 on the education sector. The procedures recommended by employers and the guidance provided by the main teaching unions are also examined in some detail.

In chapter 9, Jennifer Frieze and Karen Jennings look at the background to the PIDA 1998 and draw upon the experience of high-profile cases that occurred in the public services during the 1990s. The authors then examine what the new legislation means for trade unions and discuss the importance of whistleblowing policies and procedures. This is followed by a detailed analysis of the advice unions give to their representatives on negotiating whistleblowing procedures and on how to assist members to raise concerns. The authors also consider the benefits to union organization of developing good practice around whistleblowing. The chapter concludes with a discussion of some of the potential problems that PIDA 1998 poses for trade unions.

In chapter 10 Kate Schroder suggests that, in the light of recent research, gaps remain in the legal protection afforded to whistleblowers. She maintains that the current legislation has failed to take into account fully the lessons to be learned from the actual experiences of whistleblowers. Her research demonstrates that workers and employers may take steps to prevent damage sustained through whistleblowing but that this largely depends upon the implementation of suitable reporting procedures and a willingness to make appropriate changes to workplace culture. The case studies identified in the author's research cover all sectors and many different occupations. By analysing whistleblowers' experiences, the author believes that it is possible to minimize some of the negative effects of whistleblowing. The chapter makes recommendations which are based on the sample of cases referred to and the author's personal experience of whistleblowing.

The final chapter was written by Chidi King. It recognizes that, although workers have often been at the fore of uncovering organizational wrongdoing, this has usually been at great personal cost to themselves and their families. Until recently the law had ignored the role that diligent employees could play in safeguarding the public interest and offered little protection to those who hit out at corporate malpractice. Additionally, although some trade unions were alive to the issue and provided invaluable support to their members, there was a noticeable absence of readily available independent advice and assistance for those who were wrestling with the question of whether or not to 'blow the whistle'. The launch of Public Concern at Work in 1993 provided that resource and the charity became a driving force behind the enactment of PIDA 1998. This chapter examines the help currently available in the United Kingdom to both employers and potential whistleblowers. It also draws on PCAW's own research and casework in order to provide useful guidance to workers on whether and how to 'blow the whistle'.

NOTES

1. Nader, Ralph, Petkas, P.J. and Blackwell, K. (eds), *Whistleblowing: The Report of the Conference on Professional Responsibility*, New York, Bantam, 1972.
2. Senate Select Committee on Public Interest Whistleblowing, *In the Public Interest*, AGPS, Canberra, 1994, paragraph 2.2. For other definitions see Jubb, Peter, 'Whistleblowing: a restrictive definition and interpretation', *Journal of Business Ethics*, 1999, pp. 77–94.
3. Senate Select Committee on Public Interest Whistleblowing, *In the Public Interest*, AGPS, Canberra, 1994, paragraph 2.12.
4. It should be acknowledged that some writers do not accept that internal disclosures amount to whistleblowing: see Jubb, Peter, 'Whistleblowing: a restrictive definition and interpretation', *Journal of Business Ethics*, 1999, pp. 77–94.
5. Micelli, M. and Near, J. *Blowing the whistle*, New York, Lexington Books, 1992.
6. On the compatibility of whistleblowing with notions of employee loyalty: see Larmer, Robert, 'Whistleblowing and employee loyalty', *Journal of Business Ethics*, 1992, pp. 125–8.
7. See: the False Claims Act 1986 (USA) and the rewards offered by the Inland Revenue and Customs and Excise in the UK.
8. See: Sims, Randi and Keenan, John, 'Predictors of external whistleblowing: organisational and intrapersonal variable', *Journal of Business Ethics*, 1998, pp. 411–21.
9. See: Public Concern at Work, *The Police*, London, 1993.
10. Department of Transport, *Court of Enquiry No.8074*, London, HMSO, 1987.
11. *Public inquiry into the Piper Alpha Disaster*, CM 1310, London, HMSO, 1990.
12. Vickers, Lucy, *Protecting whistleblowers at work*, London, Institute of Employment Rights, 1995.
13. For a useful discussion of the social/psychological dimensions of whistleblowing see: Gobert, James and Punch, Maurice, 'Whistleblowers, the public interest, and the Public Interest Disclosure Act 1998', *Modern Law Review*, 2000, pp. 25–54.
14. For a brief survey of other jurisdictions see: Bowers, John, Mitchell, Jack and Lewis, Jeremy *Whistleblowing: The New Law*, London, Sweet & Maxwell, 1999, Appendix 8.

2
The Law Relating to Whistleblowing
DAVID LEWIS & MAUREEN SPENCER

In this chapter we examine the laws which inhibit the disclosure of information by workers and those which encourage it. In particular, we discuss the extent to which the Public Interest Disclosure Act 1998 (henceforward PIDA 1998) protects whistleblowers in certain circumstances. Finally, we consider the position of whistleblowers as witnesses in court proceedings.[1]

CONSTRAINTS ON DISCLOSURE

Workers have never had a general right to disclose information about their employment. Even the revelation of *non-confidential* material could be regarded as undermining the implied duty of trust and confidence and give rise to an action for breach of contract. Indeed, prior to the implementation of the PIDA 1998, express terms were extensively used to prevent any external discussion of an employer's activities (so-called 'gagging clauses' are discussed below on page 11).

In relation to *confidential* information obtained in the course of employment, the common law again provides protection against disclosure through both express and implied terms. The duty of fidelity can be used to prevent disclosures while the employment subsists and express terms (restrictive covenants) can be used to inhibit the activities of former employees after the relationship has ceased. However, post-employment restraints will only be enforceable if they can be shown to protect legitimate business interests and are reasonable in all the circumstances. Where employees have allegedly disclosed confidential information in breach of an express or implied term they may seek to invoke a public interest defence to a legal action. Although the common law allows the public interest to be used as a shield against an injunction or damages, we will see that it is a weapon of uncertain strength.

Since the case of *Initial Services v Putterill [1968] 1 QB 396*, the

Court of Appeal has allowed an exception to the principle of non-disclosure of confidential information where there is 'any misconduct of such a nature that it ought in the public interest to be disclosed to others'. Here a sales manager was sued for breach of confidence to stop him passing documents relating to unlawful price-fixing to a national newspaper. However,the disclosure must be to someone who has an interest in receiving it and, in this case, Lord Denning was of the opinion that the media had a sufficient interest for these purposes.

In *Lion Laboratories v Evans [1985] QB 526*, two employees gave a national newspaper copies of internal documents doubting the reliability of the breathalysers manufactured by their employer. The company sought an injunction to prevent publication of the information on the grounds of breach of confidence. The action failed because the employees were found to have 'just cause or excuse' for disclosure. However,the Court of Appeal indicated that the press might not always be the appropriate medium for disclosure.

Subsequently, in *Re a Company's Application [1989] IRLR 477*, the High Court refused to grant an injunction preventing an employee in the financial services sector from disclosing confidential information about his company to a regulatory body, notwithstanding that the disclosure might be motivated by malice. Although Mr Justice Scott continued an injunction against general disclosure, he held that an employee's duty of confidence did not prevent them disclosing to regulatory authorities matters which it was within the province of those authorities to investigate. (Such regulatory authorities are likely to be 'prescribed persons' for the purposes of PIDA 1998 see below.)

A particular inhibiting factor was the widespread insertion of so-called 'gagging clauses' into work contracts. Such clauses expressly prohibited the disclosure of information acquired during employment and caused particular confusion when placed alongside codes of conduct which encouraged the internal reporting of malpractices. However, Section 43J of the Employment Rights Act 1996 (henceforward ERA 1996) now renders void any provision in an agreement which 'purports to preclude the worker from making a protected disclosure'. This section impacts on both work contracts and agreements to settle legal proceedings but will not apply to matters which fall outside the definition of a 'qualifying disclosure'.[2]

According to Section 43B(1) ERA 1996, a 'qualifying disclosure' is one which a worker reasonably believes tends to show one or more of the following: a criminal offence; a failure to comply with any legal obligation; a miscarriage of justice; danger to the health and safety of any individual; damage to the environment; or the deliberate concealment of information tending to show any of the matters listed above. Thus a clause which prevented the disclosure of information about a type of wrongdoing which is not listed in Section 43B(1) ERA 1996 would still be enforceable. For example,an express term could restrain disclosures about mismanagement (so long as it did not amount to a criminal or civil law wrong) but not unlawful maladministration. Nevertheless Section 43J ERA 1996 may make it easier for those who are bound by professional codes of practice (for example, public service accountants, health visitors, nurses and midwives) to reconcile their contractual and professional obligations (see chapters 4 and 6 respectively on accountancy and the health service).

Another potential constraint has been the imposition of short and fixed-term employment contracts.[3] For example, in the offshore oil and gas industries many workers have been employed on two-week contracts. Given management's almost unfettered discretion whether or not to renew a contract, no doubt many workers felt inhibited about making unauthorized disclosures of information. However, Section 103A ERA 1996, which applies irrespective of a complainant's age or length of service, now makes it automatically unfair to dismiss employees on the grounds that they have made a protected disclosure. (For these purposes, the expiry of a fixed-term contract 'without being renewed under the same contract' amounts to a dismissal.) Alternatively,workers who cannot claim unfair dismissal because they do not have a contract of employment can complain under Section 47B ERA 1996 that they have been subjected to a detriment for making a protected disclosure. In these circumstances Section 48(2) ERA 1996 obliges the employer to show the grounds for non-renewal. Of course, determined employers may try to invent potentially fair reasons for ending the relationship (for example, relating to conduct, capability, redundancy, etc.) and much will depend on the vigilance of employment tribunals. However,it will no longer be enough simply to assert that those who have raised concerns are unsuitable for further employment.

Thus, apart from the situation where an employee reports a breach of statutory duty to a relevant regulatory body, the common law has not provided reliable guidelines about what could be disclosed and to whom.[4] Certainly it afforded little protection for those who are penalized by their employer for disclosing in the public interest. Pressure exerted on a whistle-blower may be regarded as breaching the employer's duty to maintain trust and confidence. However, since the employer can also argue that the disclosure itself destroyed trust and confidence, it is highly unlikely that a court would order specific performance of the contract. As regards damages, an employee could expect to be compensated for pecuniary losses arising from a breach of contract, for example, if there was a wrongful dismissal. Nevertheless, employees are unlikely to be successful claiming for non-pecuniary losses suffered as a result of making a disclosure in the public interest, for example if the employer fails to show respect for the employee.

Finally, the potential role of the law of defamation should not be underestimated. Assuming there has been sufficient publication, a whistleblower may be sued on the basis that his or her allegations were defamatory. If defamation proceedings are commenced, it is insufficient that the whistleblower had an honest belief on reasonable grounds[5] unless they can also rely on the defence of qualified privilege, i.e. they had a legal, moral or social duty to communicate their concern and did so to a person who had an interest in receiving it. Since legal aid is not available in such proceedings, individuals may well feel inhibited if an organization threatens to seek an injunction.

ENCOURAGEMENT TO DISCLOSE PRIOR TO 1998

Whether employees have a general obligation to report the misde-meanours of fellow workers to their employer depends on the individual contract and the circumstances.[6] Thus, in *Swain v West Ltd [1936] Chanc 261* there was an express term in a manager's contract that he would do 'all in his power to promote, extend and develop the interests of the company'. The Court of Appeal ruled that this imposed an obligation to disclose the wrongdoing of a managing director. Similarly, in *Sybron Corporation v Rochem Ltd [1983] IRLR 253*, the Court of Appeal held that a senior executive in a multinational financial corporation had an implied duty to disclose to his employer the involvement of colleagues in a serious fraud, even if that required him to disclose his own misdeeds. Since workers are less likely to report concerns if they fear retaliation, we will now examine the circumstances in which the law provides specific protection against victimization.

Regulation 14 of the Management of the Health and Safety at Work Regulations 1999 requires employees to inform *employers* of any work situation which could be reasonably considered to represent a serious and immediate danger to health and safety, and of any shortcomings in the employer's protection arrangements which have not previously been reported. This duty is supported by Sections 44(1)(c) and 100(1)(c) of ERA 1996, which provide that, where there is no safety representative or it is not reasonably practicable to raise the matter through such a representative or a safety committee, it is unlawful to dismiss or to impose a detriment on an employee who has 'brought to his employer's attention, by reasonable means, circumstances connected with his work which he reasonably believed were harmful or potentially harmful to health and safety'.

Whereas Sections 44 and 100 ERA 1996 require employees to report their concerns internally in the first instance, Sections 104 and 104A ERA 1996 are relevant to external whistleblowing. These offer some protection to those who assert that their employer has infringed certain statutory rights. Thus a dismissal is to be regarded as unfair if the reason or principal reason for it was that the employee (i) brought proceedings against the employer to enforce a relevant statutory right; or (ii) alleged that the employer had infringed a relevant statutory right.[7] However, it should be noted that both the claim to the right and that it has been infringed must be made in good faith.

Similarly, Section 4(1) of the Sex Discrimination Act 1975 and Section 2(1) of the Race Relations Act 1976 allow a complaint to be brought where the discrimination takes place by reason that the person victimized has 'given evidence or information in connection with proceedings brought by any person against the discriminator or any other person' under the Act, or 'has alleged that the discriminator or any other person has committed an act which...- would amount to a contravention of' the Act. This protection is unavailable if the allegation made by the victim is false and not made in good faith. Thus it would seem that the section applies if the allegation was either true but made out of malice, or false but made in good faith. As we will see later, such an approach is less restrictive than the requirements for making a protected disclosure under PIDA 1998.

Prior to the implementation of the PIDA 1998,the general law of unfair dismissal provided scant protection for those making disclosures in the public interest.[8] Apart from the problem of exclusions and qualifications, a dismissal could be justified under Section 98(1) and (2) ERA 1996 either on the grounds of misconduct or 'some other substantial reason'. Assuming that a potentially fair reason could be established, Section 98(4) ERA 1996 requires a consideration of whether it was reasonable to dismiss in all the circumstances. At this stage the employment tribunal might consider a range of factors, including the employee's motive in making the disclosure and whether steps were taken to resolve the matter internally before going outside the organization. Also relevant are the general issues of warnings, consultation, consistency of treatment and the availability of alternative employment. Even if there was a finding of unfairness, an employee's desire for reinstatement or re-engagement could be frustrated easily[9] and compensation was capped.

Mention should also be made of the Human Rights Act 1998 (HRA 1998), which incorporates the European Convention on Human Rights into UK law. Article 10 of the European Convention states that: 'Everyone has the right to freedom of expession. This right shall include freedom to hold opinions and to receive and impart information and ideas without interference by public authority and regardless of frontiers.' However, Article 10(2) refers to the necessity for restrictions on this freedom in order to prevent the disclosure of confidential information. The potential value of Article 10 was highlighted in the case of journalist William Goodwin.[10] When Goodwin's magazine proposed to publish information supplied by an informant about Tetra Ltd, the company obtained an injunction. The High Court ordered Goodwin to reveal his source so that the company could take proceedings against the informant. He refused to do so and was fined £5000 for contempt. The European Court of Human Rights (ECHR) ruled that, since the company was adequately protected by the injunction, the UK courts' treatment of Goodwin constituted an interference with his freedom of expression. The ECHR was of the opinion that this particular freedom constituted one of the essential foundations of a democratic society and the safeguards to be offered to the press were of particular importance. It almost goes without saying that protection for journalists indirectly benefits whistleblowers who offer themselves as sources of information.

THE PUBLIC INTEREST DISCLOSURE ACT 1998

The purpose of this Act, which was introduced as a Private Member's Bill by the Conservative MP Richard Shepherd, is 'to protect individuals who make certain disclosures of information in the public interest'. It does so,primarily, by inserting a new Part IVA into the ERA 1996 and by making other amendments. Part IVA ERA 1996 sets out the types of disclosure which can give rise to protection (a 'qualifying disclosure'); the circumstances in which a 'qualifying disclosure' will be protected (a 'protected disclosure'); and the workers to whom the protection applies. Thus, in a sense, the approach of the common law to disclosures in the public interest has been maintained, i.e. for protection to be afforded the information must be of a particular kind and revealed to an appropriate person. What is different is that the factors to be taken into account are known in advance. Nevertheless, because there is considerable imprecision in the legislation, much will depend on the interpretation given by employment tribunals.

We have seen on page 12 that Section 43B(1) ERA 1996 defines a 'qualifying disclosure' very broadly. The six categories are not restricted to confidential information and there is no requirement for any link between what is revealed and the worker's employment. Indeed, the matter disclosed may have occurred in the past, be currently occurring or likely to occur, and relate to events outside the UK. The main restriction is that a disclosure will not qualify if the worker 'commits an offence by making it'. Clearly, while the Official Secrets Act 1989 remains on the statute book breaches will not be treated as being in the public interest!

We now turn to the potential recipients of information and the requirements that must be fulfilled for a 'qualifying disclosure' to become a 'protected disclosure'. Section 43C(1) ERA 1996 protects workers who make qualifying disclosures in good faith to their employer or to another person who is responsible for the matter disclosed. On the assumption that internal disclosures are preferable, Part IVA of ERA 1996 provides incentives for employers to introduce procedures for reporting concerns but does not oblige them to do so. In the light of recent health and safety disasters and financial scandals,it has been argued that whistleblowing procedures should be mandatory.[11]

The requirement of 'good faith' will oblige workers to show that they acted honestly. Two main questions arise from making employment protection dependent on the worker's motive (the issue of personal gain is dealt with below). First,is it not foreseeable that the possibility of motive being examined will deter some important disclosures, for example, in relation to serious crime? Second, if motive is relevant, would it not be better to require the employer to prove that the worker had acted in bad faith? It could be argued that, if a worker reasonably believes that the information is true, the motive for reporting should be disregarded. This would not necessarily expose employers to great harm. Malicious allegations could be deterred by making it a serious disciplinary offence to report a concern where there were no reasonable grounds for believing that the information supplied was accurate (see chapter 5 on the possible contents of a whistleblowing procedure).

Section 43D ERA 1996 encourages workers who have a concern to seek assistance by providing that a disclosure will be protected if it is made in the course of obtaining legal advice. Solicitor–client relationships are also reinforced by Section 43B(4) ERA 1996. This provides that where information has been given to a person in the course of obtaining legal advice, and the information would be subject to professional privilege in legal proceedings, disclosure by that person will not be protected. Although PIDA 1998 does not create an advice-giving agency, we would argue that a specialist body should be established. (See chapter 11 on the services provided by Public Concern at Work.) Such a body could ensure that advisory and counselling services are available and educate the public about the legitimacy of reporting concerns in a democratic society.

Section 43E ERA 1996 protects workers in government-appointed organizations (e.g. non-departmental public bodies) if they make a disclosure in good faith to the sponsor department rather than their legal employer. It is worth noting that the Minister, like other designated recipients under the PIDA 1998, has no duty to take any action in relation to matters which may be disclosed. Nevertheless, those who have knowledge of potential wrongdoing may be held liable for culpable inaction under both the civil and criminal law, for example, in relation to health and safety matters.

Section 43F(1) ERA 1996 protects workers who make disclosures in good faith to a person (or class of persons) prescribed for the purpose by the Secretary of State.[12] However, the worker must reasonably believe that: (i) the matter falls within the remit of the prescribed person; and (ii) that the information and any allegation contained in it are substantially true. As regards (ii), we would argue that the public interest may not be served if workers are deterred by the requirement to demonstrate their reasonable belief in the 'substantial truth' of information and allegations. In addition, workers cannot report what they have been told by another person unless they themselves reasonably believe that there is a qualifying disclosure. This is designed to ensure that the prescribed persons are not overwhelmed by hearsay and anecdotal evidence.

Section 43G ERA 1996 enables workers to make a protected disclosure to outsiders in other limited circumstances. Parliament's preference for disclosures to be made to employers or prescribed persons is highlighted by the number and nature of the hurdles that must be overcome for protection to be afforded by this section. Workers must: (i) act in good faith; (ii) reasonably believe that the information and any allegation contained in it are substantially true; (iii) not act for personal gain; (iv) have already disclosed substantially the same information to the employer or to a person prescribed under Section 43F ERA 1996, unless they reasonably believe that they would be subject to a detriment for doing so, or that the employer would conceal or destroy the evidence if alerted; (v) act reasonably. In assessing reasonableness, regard shall be had, in particular, to: (a) the identity of the person to whom the disclosure is made; (b) the seriousness of the matter; (c) whether there is a continuing failure or one likely to recur; (d) whether the disclosure is made in breach of a duty of confidentiality owed by the employer to another person; (e) any action the employer (or prescribed person) has taken or might have been expected to take in relation to a previous disclosure; and (f) whether the worker has complied with any procedure authorized by the employer for making a disclosure.

The issue of disclosing for personal gain is problematic. Since there is a separate requirement to demonstrate good faith, it is clear that this is not being used as a test of the worker's motive. The possibility that personal and public interests might coincide is recognized, to some extent, by Section 43L(2) ERA 1996. This states that for these purposes a reward payable under any enactment will be disregarded.[13] Chequebook journalism may not be desirable but, if a financial incentive enables one disaster to be avoided, isn't disclosure in the public interest? We would argue that, if all the other requirements of Section 43G ERA 1996 are satisfied, it may not be appropriate to oblige workers to prove that their purpose was not personal gain.

Section 43H ERA 1996 deals with disclosures about exceptionally serious failures. In order to be protected workers must fulfil the first three requirements of Section 43G ERA 1996 (above). In addition, the relevant failure must be of an exceptionally serious nature and it must be reasonable in all the circumstances to make the disclosure. Again Parliament's concern that disclosures should be no wider than necessary is emphasized by reference, in particular, to the identity of the recipient in determining reasonableness. It would defeat the object of this catch-all section if failures of an exceptionally serious nature were defined by statute. However, the effect is that these will be determined by employment tribunals and the courts on a case-by-case basis. Thus, as with the common law, workers will learn *only after the event* whether their disclosures were protected.

Section 43K(1) ERA 1996 is designed to enable everyone who works to benefit from Part IVA ERA 1996, irrespective of whether they fall within the definition of 'employee' or 'worker' contained in Section 230 ERA 1996. Section 43K(2) ERA 1996 extends the definition of 'employer' accordingly. We would argue that granting employment protection rights to the widest range of people is desirable as a matter of principle.[14]

Section 47B(1) ERA 1996 provides the right not to be subjected to any detriment 'on the ground that the worker has made a protected disclosure'. A major concern here is whether tribunals will interpret this section purposively by applying it to those who have been penalized for 'attempting to make' a protected disclosure. If they do not, the consequences could be grave - employers will have an incentive to victimize those who are in the process of exposing misdeeds but have not completed the procedure.[15] Although Section 47B(1) ERA 1996 does not deal with a detriment imposed by someone who has no direct relationship with the worker, workers may complain that their employer has subjected them to a detriment by failing to protect them from the actions of third parties (e.g. another employer).

Section 103A ERA 1996 makes it automatically unfair to dismiss employees on the grounds that they have made a protected disclosure. Similarly, Section 105(6A) ERA 1996 makes it unfair to select employees for redundancy if the reason for doing so is that they have made a protected disclosure. In both situations the normal qualifying period of service and the upper age limit do not apply. In addition, Section 237(1A) TULRCA 1992 is amended so that an employee who is taking part in an unofficial strike or other unofficial industrial action who is dismissed for making a protected disclosure can complain of unfair dismissal. Interim relief is provided for and Section 124(1A) ERA 1996 allows unlimited compensation to be awarded for dismissal contrary to Section 103A or 105(6A) ERA 1996.

In relation to general exclusions and qualifications, it should be noted that Part IVA ERA 1996 applies to Crown employees who are not subject to a certificate exempting them on grounds of national security. However, it does not currently apply to the security services or those who have a contract of employment in the police service.

WHISTLEBLOWERS AS WITNESSES IN COURT PROCEEDINGS

Whether or not they are protected by PIDA 1998, workers who make disclosures of wrongdoing may be called as witnesses in civil or criminal proceedings. Thus they may be open to possible reprisals by employers, particularly because any anonymity they may have been able to safeguard previously will be threatened. If employers attempt to prevent evidence being given in court they may face action for contempt or other specific offences. Intimidation of witnesses itself may be contempt of court and, in the most serious cases, will amount to the offence of perverting the course of justice.

In Attorney-General v Butterworth [1963] 1QB 696 the Court of Appeal held that victimizing a witness after he had given evidence amounts to contempt of court. Mr Greenlees, a member of the National Federation of Retail Newsagents, Booksellers and Stationers gave evidence before the Restrictive Practices Tribunal about the Federation's agreement with the Newspaper Proprietors' Association, claiming that it was harmful to the public. This antagonized his fellow members and he was expelled from the Federation. The Court of Appeal held that contempt of court was not confined to pending cases. Victimization of a witness was an interference with the proper administration of justice because it might deter potential witnesses from giving evidence in future cases. *In Peach Grey & Co v Sommers [1995] IRLR 363*, the High Court offered protection to a victimized witness in employment tribunal proceedings by holding that the courts had power to punish for contempt in accordance with Order 52 of the Rules of the Supreme Court.

A more specific action against a punitive employer may be afforded by Section 51 of the Criminal Justice and Public Order Act 1994, which makes witness intimidation a criminal offence. In its wording it could apply to those who suffer financial disadvantage such as loss of a job. Intimidation is defined as acts or threats to harm someone, physically or financially, and includes acts or threats against a third party, for example, a relative of the person being targeted. The act or threat must be intended to intimidate and the perpetrator must know or believe that the other person is helping or has helped an investigation, or is a witness or potential witness. The perpetrator must have acted or threatened the person because they believed this and had the intention of obstructing the course of justice. Under this Act such intention is presumed unless the contrary is proven.

It is sometimes suggested that, in order to prevent reprisals being taken against them, witnesses should be allowed to give evidence anonymously. Since the principle of open justice is extremely important,only very rarely is this allowed in court. Informants who are not called as witnesses may be protected, since there is a public policy interest in maintaining the flow of information on wrongdoing to statutory bodies. Thus in *D v National Society for the Prevention of Cruelty to Children [1978] AC 171* the court refused to reveal the identity of people who volunteered information about child cruelty to the NSPCC. However, the case of *A v Company B [1997] IRLR 405* demonstrates that whistle-blowers who wish to remain anonymous may have difficulties in certain circumstances. Here an employee was dismissed as a result of evidence of alleged wrongdoing being given to his employer. He successfully applied for discovery by the employer of the infor-mant's identity so that he could initiate defamation proceedings.

One means of shielding whistleblowers is to allow them to give evidence by written document, admissible as an exception to the rule against hearsay evidence in criminal proceedings. Under Section 24 of the Criminal Justice Act 1988 business documents are generally admissible without a reason for not calling the witness. However, where the document is prepared for the purposes of pending or contemplated criminal proceedings or a criminal investigation, there has to be an acceptable reason. Thus, for example, if a statement is made to the Health and Safety Executive by a worker who has first-hand knowledge of the circumstances, it may be admissible at a subsequent criminal trial without calling the witness to give oral evidence if they fear for their position at work.

CONCLUSION

If the public interest in protecting whistleblowers was never clearly articulated prior to the PIDA 1998, this legislation attempts to do so, albeit in a restrictive fashion.[16] We have noted that PIDA 1998 offers nothing to citizens who wish to report employer wrong-doing but do not have the status of being a 'worker'. For less obvious reasons, the legislation fails to deal with discrimination at the hiring stage against those who have made a protected disclo-sure. Although cynics will argue that victimization in the recruit-ment process can easily be concealed, Parliament has marked its disapproval in relation to discrimination on the grounds of sex, race, disability and trade union membership. In our opinion, workers should have the right to complain about any situation in which they believe they have been victimized for making (or attempting to make) a protected disclosure.

Although Lord Nolan commended the PIDA 1998 'for so skil-fully achieving the essential but delicate balance...between the public interest and the interests of employers', it could be argued that in reality employers' interests have been given priority. Of course, it remains to be seen how the PIDA 1988 will operate in practice and whether it will be bolstered by the implementation of the Human Rights Act 1998 and the proposed Freedom of Information Act. Section 3(1) of the HRA 1998 requires employment tribunals to give effect to primary and subordinate legislation in a way which is compatible with the European Convention on Human Rights 'so far as it is possible to do so'. In addition, it will make it 'unlawful for a public authorities to act in a way that is incompatible with a Convention right' (see page 15 above on freedom of expression). One possibility is that workers employed by public authorities will be able to use both the PIDA 1988 and the HRA 1988 to justify their disclosures.

NOTES

1. For a detailed analysis of the current legal position see Bowers, John, Mitchell, Jack and Lewis, Jeremy, *Whistleblowing: the new law*, London, 1999.
2. On the enforceability of secrecy agreements in the USA see: Dworkin, Terry and Callahan, Elletta, 'Buying silence', *American Business Law Journal*, 1998, p. 1594.
3. An EU Directive aimed at preventing abuses arising from successive fixed-term contracts is due to be implemented by Member States by 28 June 2001.
4. It should be noted that if the police acquire confidential information, which in their reasonable view, is in the interests of public health and safety, should be considered by a professional or regulatory body, then they are entitled to give that information to such a body whether or not it was requested: see *Woolgar v Chief Constable of Sussex [1999] 3 AER 604*.
5. A claim for malicious falsehood cannot succeed if a whistleblower had an honest belief that an allegation was true.
6. It should also be noted that Section 93A of the Criminal Justice Act 1993 imposes a duty on 'all persons' to report money laundering.
7. The relevant statutory rights include those conferred by the ERA 1996 which can be exercised at an employment tribunal; some sections of the Trade Union and Labour Relations (Consolidation) Act 1992 and rights conferred by the Working Time Regulations 1998.
8. The general law of unfair dismissal still applies if a person is sacked for making a disclosure which is not 'protected' within the meaning of the PIDA 1998.
9. Not only must employment tribunals be persuaded that it would be practicable to order re-employment but the employer could simply choose to pay additional compensation rather than comply with any order: see Sections 116 and 117 ERA 1996.

10. See *Goodwin v United Kingdom [1996] 22 EHRR 123.*

11. See: Lewis,David 'Whistleblowers and job security', *Modern Law Review*, 1995, pp. 208–21.

12. The Schedule to the Public Interest Disclosure (Prescribed Persons) Order 1999 S.I.1549 specifies the persons prescribed and the description of matters in respect of which they are prescribed.

13. Recent US Federal Statutes and some State laws which provide protection for whistleblowers encourage reports of wrongdoing by offering rewards.

14. Section 23 of the Employment Relations Act 1999 gives the Secretary of State the power to confer rights on individuals.

15. It is worth noting that several US State statutes protect so-called 'embryonic whistleblowers'.

16. For general assessments of PIDA 1998 see: Lewis, David 'The Public Interest Disclosure Act 1998', *Industrial Law Journal*, 1998, pp. 325–30 and Gobert, James and Punch, Maurice 'Whistleblowers, the public interest, nd the Public Interest Disclosure Act 1998', *Modern Law Review*, 2000, pp. 25–54.

3

Whistleblowing and Business Ethics

TONY CUTLER AND DAVID NYE

INTRODUCTION

This chapter discusses whistleblowing within a theoretical framework of two approaches to corporate social responsibility which
appear to be radically different. The 'stakeholder' approach regards
corporate entities as responsible to a range of 'stakeholders' including, for example, shareholders, workers and customers. By way of
contrast, there is the 'shareholder agent' or 'classical' approach,
which argues that corporate managers are agents of shareholders
and solely responsible to that group. This distinction is relevant to
the treatment of whistleblowing in business ethics because situations where whistleblowing occurs commonly involve information
held by agents of a business whose disclosure could be seen as in
the interests of some stakeholders but which would simultaneously
damage corporate financial performance. Such information might,
for example, involve issues relating to health and safety, product
risks to consumers or the price and quality of goods and services.
The aim of the chapter is to show that while the two approaches
have different implications for the ethics of whistleblowing, this
distinction is much less clear cut if the ethical underpinnings of
the 'classical' view are explained.

The chapter is divided into five sections. The first compares the
'stakeholder' and 'shareholder agent' approaches and outlines their
implications for whistleblowing. In this discussion the 'shareholder
agent' approach is represented by Milton Friedman, who is
'perhaps the best-known exponent of the classical view'.[1] An initial
reading of Friedman's position is advanced which we call 'Friedman I'. In the second section, the 'stakeholding' approach and
'Friedman I' are applied to two business situations, both involving
non-disclosure of information relevant to the assessment of risks
by workers and consumers. Our objective here is to illustrate how

and why the two approaches differ in their evaluation of the ethics of whistleblowing. In the third section, Friedman's argument is re-examined and an attempt is made to produce a more sophisticated interpretation which analyses the underlying conceptual framework of his argument. This reading, which Friedman himself does not develop,leads to a different view of corporate social responsibility which we categorize as 'Friedman II.' In the fourth section, 'Friedman II' is used to analyse the two business settings described earlier and conclusions are drawn which are different to those suggested by the 'classical' view. The final section locates 'stakeholding' approaches and 'Friedman II' in wider ethical frameworks and considers their implications for the debate about whether or not there is a duty to blow the whistle.

STAKEHOLDING AND SHAREHOLDER AGENT CONCEPTS OF CORPORATE SOCIAL RESPONSIBILITY

STAKEHOLDING

The 'stakeholding' concept of corporate social responsibility is based on the idea that a business corporation and its agents are ethically responsible to a plurality of groups. The inclusion of such groups relates to the claim that they all have an interest in the operation of business corporations. For example, shareholders as legal owners have an interest in financial returns both in terms of earnings and capital growth. Workers have an interest in the terms and conditions of employment, including job security and safety at work. Consumers have an interest in the quality and safety of products and local communities have an interest in, for example, the impact of corporations on local employment and the environment. Consequently, each of these groups is seen as having a 'stake' in the business and therefore their interests ought to be considered in corporate decision-making. Thus Evan and Freeman argue 'the very purpose of the firm is, in our view, to serve as a vehicle for coordinating stakeholder interests'.[2]

This approach has one obvious implication for whistleblowing. Where there is a contradiction between a stakeholder interest in the disclosure of information and corporate financial performance, a stakeholding position cannot justify opposition to disclosure of such information simply on the grounds that a weaker financial performance will damage shareholder interests. This is because shareholders are just one of the stakeholders and cannot be presumed to have interests which take priority over the other stakeholders. Thus, while Evan and Freeman state that returns to shareholders are required as 'their support is necessary for the survival of the firm and they have a legitimate claim on the firm', this implies no priority for shareholder interests since 'similar reasoning applies...to each stakeholder group'.[3] Stakeholding approaches raise many difficulties. For example, it is often unclear how the diverse interests of the stakeholder groups are to be considered and balanced. Arguably, however, there is a presumption in favour of whistleblowing because the corporation is seen as serving a broad public interest encompassing a plurality of groups each of which have a 'stake' in it.

THE SHAREHOLDER–AGENT CONCEPT

A radically different approach to corporate social responsibility is apparently taken by Friedman. Modern business corporations reflect a distinction between ownership and control, at least in the sense that the vast majority of shareholders are not involved in corporate strategic or operational decision-making. The latter is the preserve of managers. According to Friedman, such managers are agents of the principal, the shareholder. Thus, he argues, 'in a free-enterprise, private-property system, a corporate executive is an employee of the owners of the business. He has direct responsibility to his employers. That responsibility is to conduct the business in accordance with their desires.'[4] Hence the appropriate role of the corporate executive is to act as an agent of the shareholder. Furthermore, while some corporate bodies may be non profit-making, the norm is that the 'desires' of shareholders will be to 'make as much money as possible'.

Friedman indicates that there are certain restrictions on the methods the agent may use. Thus he states that financial returns should be pursued 'while conforming to the basic rules of society'. These are said to be 'those embodied in law and those embodied in ethical custom'. At this point Friedman does not specify the content of 'ethical custom', although later he is somewhat more precise (see below). Nevertheless, it is clear in his argument that the pursuit of financial returns must be within the framework of law as the embodiment of 'the basic rules of society'. It is this obligation to pursue financial targets within the framework of law which we designate the 'Friedman I' theory of corporate social responsibility.

Notwithstanding such limitations, 'Friedman I' implies a negative view of whistleblowing in ethical terms. As indicated above, whistleblowing can be controversial and trigger hostility because of its implications for corporate financial performance. Moreover, the avoidance of damage to financial performance is seen in 'Friedman I' as the principal duty of the agent. Thus justifications for whistleblowing which emphasize stakeholder interests are irrelevant as there is only one group (shareholders) whose interests have to be considered. To illustrate the difference between the approaches of 'Friedman I' and stakeholder theory, we now examine two business settings which involve product risks to either consumers or workers and analyse the implications for whistleblowing.

TWO BUSINESS SCENARIOS

THE VELSICOL CASE

The US chemical company, Velsicol, manufactured two pesticides, Chlordane and Heptachlor. Initially these pesticides were used in both agriculture and in the treatment of houses. However, the US Environmental Protection Agency (henceforward EPA) prohibited their use in agriculture because of the carcinogenicity of both products.[5] The use of both pesticides in treating houses was continued until 1988 when, under an agreement between Velsicol and the EPA, both products were withdrawn from commercial use in the USA. Evidence from internal sources points to company knowledge of the carcinogenic character of both products prior to the 1974 ban in agriculture. A transcript of a conversation between two Velsicol executives included the statement that, if test data available to the company were submitted to the EPA, the latter would 'suspend registration of the agricultural uses for chlordane and heptachlor'. This material, and other relevant data indicating the carcinogenic risks of the products in such uses were *not* submitted to the EPA.

After 1974 the use of the two pesticides in houses was allowed because of the EPA's acceptance of assurances that subterranean applications would not involve human exposure. However, in

1973 the US Air Force reported to Velsicol that 800 homes on an air base treated in 1972 had been contaminated. This incident led the US National Academy of Sciences to recommend the collection of epidemiological data on inhabitants of the homes treated. Velsicol failed to act on this or subsequent recommendations to carry out such studies. There was also evidence of risks to workers as government scientists had demonstrated excess cancer mortality rates in those engaged in the manufacture of chlordane. Equally, Velsicol product labels failed 'to disclose the presence of a variety of toxic and carcinogenic ingredients, additives and contaminants'. It is also worth noting that export of the products continued to twenty-five countries after the 1988 ban in the USA and that the product continued to be used in agriculture as late as 1989.

From a stakeholding perspective, an argument can be made for whistleblowing in this situation. Workers and consumers were being put at risk from these products and the nature of these risks was not appropriately conveyed in labelling. The company both suppressed relevant information and failed to follow recommendations that data be gathered which could have revealed risks. The product continued to be sold in export markets even after the total ban in the USA, although it could be argued that there is no ethical warrant to discriminate between domestic and foreign product users.[6] Naturally, in a stakeholding approach, interests have to be balanced. Thus the possible pecuniary losses of shareholders and the potential threat to the job security of workers would have to be taken into account. However, these interests might be seen as weighing less than the risks of morbidity and premature mortality to customers and workers stemming from the manufacture and application of the product.

From the 'Friedman I' standpoint, a quite different set of conclusions can be drawn. According to the principal–agent relationship, keeping a profitable commercial item in production serves the principal's financial interest and is in line with the agent's duty. This *was* regarded as a relevant consideration by Velsicol executives. Thus, in the transcript referred to above, the following remark was made with respect to withdrawing the products: 'Heptachlor, I would say, wouldn't be a great impact because they're only projecting something like a million pounds total for all of next year, worldwide. Chlordane's a different matter, a far different matter.'[7] Thus shareholder agency arguments would suggest a duty to keep the items in production. Equally, the company was operating within the law. Although Velsicol was indicted in 1977 for, *inter alia*, concealing material facts from the EPA, the case was dismissed on procedural grounds.

'LOW TAR', 'LOW NICOTINE' CIGARETTES

The second business scenario is drawn from the tobacco industry and differs from the Velsicol case in one important respect. In Velsicol consumers and workers were unaware of the product risks because of suppression of information. In the case of 'low tar' and 'low nicotine' cigarettes smokers are aware of the risks involved but wish to minimize them by consuming a distinct variety of the product. Thus some smokers have sought to protect their health, while continuing to smoke, by switching to brands with a lower tar yield.

Tar and nicotine yields (which are given in milligrams) are now displayed on packet labels and/or advertisements in most regulatory regimes. They are calculated by collecting and weighing the amount of nicotine drawn when a machine 'smokes' cigarettes according to a predetermined programme. Thus yield ratings are considered to be an index of the relative 'strength' and toxicity of different brands. For example, everything else being equal, smokers of a 10 mg tar cigarette will, by switching to a 5 mg tar cigarette, reduce their tar intake by 50 per cent. Similarly, their nicotine intake would drop in proportion to the change in the nicotine yield ratings.

Prior to the 1960s and the reports of the American Surgeon General and the Royal College of Physicians on the risks of smoking, knowledge of yields was normally confined to 'insiders' in the tobacco industry. However, subsequently there developed both regulatory and consumer pressure on tobacco manufacturers to publish yield ratings and to introduce increasingly lower yield brands. This placed the manufacturers in a dilemma. On the one hand, they could not afford to be unresponsive. On the other hand, they foresaw the possibility that smokers might ultimately reject new brands because they would fail to deliver the tar and nicotine levels required to give the smoker sufficient satisfaction. In addition, there was the possibility that the stimulation provided by lower yielding cigarettes might fall below the threshold level required to 'capture' new recruits to smoking. Market considerations of this character significantly influenced the manufacturers' decision 'to modify the products in such a way that they did not lose their appeal'.[8]

Hence research within the industry became increasingly focused on developing product design strategies which gave lower yield ratings yet facilitated the smoker's customary intake levels. One example of such a design strategy concerned tip ventilation. The amount of tar and nicotine drawn from a cigarette is proportionate to the volume of air pulled through the cigarette's burning cone. Tip ventilation consists of a band or bands of microscopic holes on the filter. The greater the degree of tip ventilation, the more air per puff is drawn through the ventilation holes and therefore the less is available to be drawn through the tobacco column. Thus, everything else being equal, lower machine-measured yield ratings are associated with higher levels of tip ventilation. Crucial to the potential ethical problems posed by tip ventilation is the difference between 'smoking' by the machine used to generate the published yield figures and the way in which people actually smoke cigarettes. Unlike the machine, smokers tend to block the ventilation holes either with their fingers or with their lips. The effect is that smokers draw more tar and nicotine than might be anticipated from the yield rating. This means that the smoker switching to a lower yielding cigarette obtains a much smaller drop in intake than would be predicted from a comparison of the published yield figures of the original brand and that to which the smoker has changed. It is clear from internal industry documents that design strategies (such as tip ventilation) have been deliberately pursued with the objective of maintaining the industry's financial performance by seeking to ensure that 'health-conscious' smokers continued to consume cigarettes. This raises the question of how whistleblowing would be regarded from the standpoint of the two approaches outlined above.

From the stakeholder perspective, there would appear to be a prima facie case for whistleblowing on grounds which are analogous to those in the Velsicol case. The manufacturers' attempt to safeguard their market is beneficial to two stakeholder groups, shareholders and workers; the former through maintaining financial returns and the latter through underpinning job security. However, the design strategy aims, and is likely to result in, a misperception of risk by the smoker because switching down will lead to a much lower reduction of intakes than anticipated. As with the Velsicol case, the nature of the risks to the groups involved are not symmetrical since, on the one side, there are financial risks but on the other risks of physical harm. Thus full disclosure could be justified on the grounds that it would give consumers a more realistic perception of the risks of smoking these products.

However, if 'Friedman I' is applied to this situation there are no grounds for whistleblowing. As with the Velsicol case, risk disclosure might damage the market for a product which had been developed partly in response to consumer demand. Furthermore, the pursuit of profit in this case does not involve any departure from the governing legal framework. Thus the law does not proscribe the design features involved. Nor does it require that information on the likely effects of the differences between yields derived from 'smoking machines' and those which would follow from the behaviour of actual smokers be published. Consequently, the strategy of the manufacturers was entirely in line with the ethical injunctions of 'Friedman I', i.e. to pursue financial returns within the framework of the law as the concrete embodiment of current social values. Thus whistleblowing in such a case would betray the obligation to the shareholder.

THE ETHICAL FOUNDATIONS OF FRIEDMAN'S ARGUMENT: 'FRIEDMAN II'

The previous section demonstrated the very different conclusions on whistleblowing which are derived from stakeholding and 'Friedman 1' approaches. However, it is worth returning to Friedman's discussion because his analysis is not without ambiguity. It was emphasized in relation to 'Friedman 1' that the pursuit of financial returns is constrained by the need to operate within the framework of law in the jurisdiction concerned. Significantly, Friedman not only includes legal constraints but also refers to 'ethical customs'. Initially, this phrase is given no particular content. However, towards the end of his argument Friedman is more precise in indicating the nature of this ethical constraint. Thus he states that the appropriate approach to corporate social responsibility is for business 'to...engage in activities designed to increase its profits so long as it stays within the rules of the game, which is to say, engages in open and fair competition without deception or fraud'.[9]

This prompts the question of what is deemed ethically problematic about 'fraud or deception'. One way this can be answered is by reference to *autonomy* as an underlying ethical value. Thus autonomy involves a respect for choice, although choice can only be exercised if it is 'informed'. Consequently, where there is 'deception or fraud' the individual is not genuinely free to choose because the decision is being made on the basis of misleading information. There is another reason why autonomy, while not being explicitly theorized, appears to be a key element in Friedman's argument – it makes sense of his insistence on the importance of the principal–agent relationship. If we ask what is wrong with the agent not carrying out the wishes of the principal (assumed by Friedman to be maximization of financial returns), then again the answer would appear to be the infringement of autonomy. Thus Friedman is claiming that shareholders (as principals) operate under the expectation that managers act as their agents. Where managers depart from their agency role by, for example, using stakeholder approaches, they are infringing the autonomy of the shareholder by deceiving them. This is the basis for what we term the 'Friedman II' approach. It suggests that what is crucial to corporate social responsibility is that autonomy ought to be respected and that this is a basic constraining condition on the pursuit of financial returns.

REVISITING THE SCENARIOS: FRIEDMAN II APPLIED

We now return to the business scenarios and suggest that quite different results emerge if 'Friedman II' is applied. Whereas with 'Friedman I' the case against whistleblowing was that the company was operating within the legal and regulatory framework of its jurisdiction, now a different test has to be applied. Namely, is the company selling or producing its product in conditions which respect the underlying value of autonomy?

In both scenarios corporate executives operated to ensure that risks were significantly understated. In the Velsicol case, this related to the information denied to both consumers and workers who had contact with the product. In relation to low-tar, low-nicotine cigarettes, information was not provided to consumers of the product. From a 'Friedman II' perspective, the companies' activities in producing and marketing the items lacks legitimacy. The relevant constraining condition is respect for autonomy and the test is whether information pertinent to the exercise of choice is or is not being revealed. In both scenarios items were being produced and sold under conditions of 'deception or fraud'. Equally, if autonomy is a key underlying value, then it is not possible to argue that a duty is owed only to shareholders. This is because, to make sense of the obligation to shareholders under 'Friedman II', it is necessary to recognize the *overarching* value of autonomy. Thus respect for autonomy must encompass *all* those who have a relationship with the corporate body, including workers and consumers. In both cases, therefore, whistleblowing would be appropriate.

WHISTLEBLOWING AND BUSINESS ETHICS

We have endeavoured to demonstrate that, notwithstanding its seminal status, Friedman's article suffers from being undertheorized in ethical terms. In business ethics, commentators frequently differ in their arguments because they subscribe to distinct theoretical traditions. The two broad traditions are utilitarianism on the one hand and deontological theories on the other. Put in highly schematic terms, the major differences can be described as follows. Utilitarian approaches are characterized by two key features. The ethical status of actions or rules/institutional practices is to be ascertained by reference to their consequences and, in turn, these are assessed on the basis of their social utility.[10] Thus many of the stakeholding arguments discussed above could be cast in these terms, since they involve identifying the consequences of practices for particular groups and then evaluating the impact on their welfare.

By way of contrast, deontological approaches focus on what are regarded as fundamental rules which govern ethical conduct and conduct is regarded as unethical insofar as it departs from these fundamental rules.[11] The argument that there is a core ethic of respect for autonomy is an instance of a deontological approach, as failure to respect autonomy will constitute *per se* an ethical wrong (whatever the attempt to justify its infringement on the grounds that benefits accrue to various groups).

It is a symptom of Friedman's undertheorization that he does not attempt explicitly to situate his argument in terms of either of these theoretical traditions. This, in part, reflects the fact that he was writing as an economist and not as an ethical theorist. However, his argument appears to fit more easily into a deontological framework. For example, it is a necessary feature of utilitarian theories that adherence to rules or institutional practices tends to be treated in a conditional way. This follows from the fact that the ethics of such practices have to be viewed in relation to their consequences. However, Friedman's argument emphasizes the duties of managers to shareholders which, although they are subject to constraining conditions, are not to be regarded as conditional. Thus the logic of Friedman's argument would appear to reject the ethical relevance of putative claims by managers that, by departing from their obligations to shareholders, they are nevertheless promoting 'social welfare'.

If, however, Friedman's views can be situated within the deontological strand of business ethics theory, it remains necessary to explore their implications for whistleblowing. One important issue which has been raised frequently in debates about the ethics of whistleblowing is how far the practice should be regarded as 'permissible' (i.e. at the discretion of the potential whistleblower) or 'obligatory' (i.e. an ethical requirement). The 'Friedman II' approach might suggest that there is an obligation. Thus, if respect for autonomy is a fundamental value which is being infringed, then it could be argued that ethical behaviour requires that this be opposed. Our analysis of the scenarios above shows that this can be done by seeking to reveal pertinent information via whistleblowing. For example, the publication of internal documents indicating both the extent of the risks and the fact that relevant information had been suppressed by corporate executives would be a means of seeking to create the conditions for genuine choice and could be regarded as an obligation for a corporate manager.

On the other hand, it has been argued that the value of respect for autonomy is that it permits the individual to live the way in which she or he chooses. Central to this approach is the idea that individual choice should be constrained only by what are termed negative duties, i.e. duties not to interfere with the autonomy of others by, for example, refraining from bodily assaults, or infringements of personal property rights. Limiting constraints in this way means that duties do not extend to aiding others. The rationale for this distinction is that if such 'positive' duties are imposed individual rights to self-determination are undermined because, in effect, individuals are at the call of 'society'. The significance of discounting positive duties is that whistleblowing can be characterized as an act of aiding others achieve informed choice. Moreover, it has been suggested that from Friedman's position duties are exclusively negative.[12] Thus the logic of 'Friedman II' would be to regard whistleblowing as permissible if there is a genuine infringement of autonomy but to reject any implication that it could be obligatory. This conclusion is similar, albeit for different reasons, to the main thrust of business ethics theory, including stakeholding approaches.

Generally contemporary theorists claim that there *is* an obligation to protect and aid others but that the stringency of this obligation has to be tempered by the cost of intervention. It is demonstrated elsewhere in this book that whistleblowers frequently face reprisals at the workplace. In part, this accounts for the predominant view in ethical theory that whistleblowing can only be regarded as obligatory in very limited circumstances. However, there is a further consideration which appears to be particularly pertinent to the premise that duties are exclusively negative in character. It is usually assumed that the individual who could give or withhold aid to another person does not stand to gain from not intervening in the situation concerned. For example, if someone witnesses a theft, a 'negative duties stance' suggests that they are not under a duty to defend the person or persons concerned. Equally, if they do not intervene they do not personally benefit from the theft. However, this would not be true in the business scenarios discussed in this chapter. As was pointed out, because non-disclosure would at least maintain corporate financial performance, there is a benefit for the corporate executive. At a minimum level this benefit could be one of increased job security but, particularly at a senior executive level, it is likely to be more extensive. Thus, it is now common for senior executives to be given options to purchase company shares so that they have a direct pecuniary interest in their appreciation.[14] This means that, unlike the classic scenarios for negative duties, the individual not giving aid (in this case by whistleblowing) is also a *beneficiary* of the infringement of autonomy concerned. It is not obvious how such situations ought to be ethically resolved, but they raise difficulties for the variety of 'Friedman II' which treats whistleblowing as simply permissible.

CONCLUSION

In this chapter we have sought to explore a paradox. While Friedman does not explicitly discuss whistleblowing, his position forms the basis for an argument that it is impermissible and that corporations are justified in punishing whistleblowers. Indeed, this is consistent with Friedman's place as a guru of free-enterprise orientated regimes such as those of Margaret Thatcher and Ronald Reagan. However, an exploration of Friedman's work shows that it contains elements (here termed 'Friedman II') which considerably extend the ethical obligations of business corporations to disclose information. In this sense the constraints of the 'rules of the game' are potentially very extensive indeed. This puts whistleblowing in a quite different light, because disclosure of information in situations where the autonomy of groups like workers or consumers is being infringed would be entirely legitimate. It is open to debate whether this can be said to generate an obligation on corporate executives to blow the whistle in such situations. However, the logic of 'Friedman II' is that they are permitted to do so. Friedman was and is a leading intellectual influence on what has been termed the 'radical right'. A closer reading of his arguments suggests that they produce a justification for whistleblowing which is 'radical' in quite a different sense.

NOTES

1. Boatright, J.R., *Ethics and the Conduct of Business*, Englewood Cliffs, New Jersey, Prentice Hall, 1997, p. 350.
2. Evan, W.M. and Freeman, W., 'A stakeholder theory of the modern corporation:Kantian capitalism' in Chryssides, G.D, and Kaler, J.H. (eds), *An Introduction to Business Ethics*, London, International Thompson Press, 1997, pp. 254–66. This article is frequently quoted and used in business ethics texts to illustrate stakeholder theory.
3. Evan, W.M. and Freeman, W., 'A stakeholder theory of the modern corporation:Kantian capitalism' in Chryssides, G.D. and Kaler, J.H. (eds), *An Introduction to Business Ethics*, London, International Thompson Press, 1997.

4. Friedman, M. 'The social responsibility of business is to increase its profits' in Adams, D.M. and Maine, E.W. (eds). *Business Ethics for the 21ˢᵗ Century*, Mountain View, California, Mayfield Publishing Co., 1998, pp. 41–5. Originally published in 1970.

5. This discussion is based on Epstein, S., 'Corporate crime: why we cannot trust industry-derived safety studies', *International Journal of Health Services*, 20, 3, p. 443.

6. Shue, H., 'Exporting hazards', *Ethics*, 91, 1981, pp. 579–606.

7. Epstein, S., 'Corporate crime: why we cannot trust industry-derived safety studies', *International Journal of Health Services*, 20, 3, p. 449.

8. Anonymous, 'Compensation for changed delivery', Minnesota Tobacco Litigation, Trial Exhibit 11.089 (www,mnbluecrosstobacco,com), p. 10.

9. Friedman, M., 'The social responsibility of business is to increase its profits' in Adams, D.M. and Maine, E.W. (eds), *Business Ethics for the 21ˢᵗ Century*, Mountain View, California, Mayfield Publishing Co., 1998, p. 12.

10. Smart, J.C. and Williams, B., *Utilitarianism, For and Against*, Cambridge, Cambridge University Press, 1980.

11. Davies, N., 'Contemporary deontology', in Singer, P. (ed.), *A Companion to Ethics*, Oxford, Blackwell, 1993, pp. 205–18.

12. Den Uyl, D.J., *The New Crusaders: The Corporate Social Responsibility Debate*, Bowling Green State University, Bowling Green, Ohio, The Social Philosophy and Policy Center, 1984, pp. 24–6.

13. Boatright, J.R., *Ethics and the Conduct of Business*, Englewood Cliffs, New Jersey, Prentice Hall, 1997, pp. 109–31.

14. Parkinson, J.E., *Corporate Power and Responsibility Issues in the Theory of Company Law*, Oxford, Oxford University Press, 1996, pp. 114–16, 221–6.

4

Whistleblowing and Accountancy

PETER SOUTHWOOD

There can be no doubt that accountants, whether in professional practice or employed within organizations of all types, face ethical conflicts from time to time. Consequently, there is a need for ethical frameworks which will assist them, in the light of legal and professional standards, to address the issues and to help them decide under what circumstances it may be justified to 'blow the whistle' where malpractice is thought to be occurring. It is hoped that this chapter will offer trainee and practising accountants a practical guide to dealing with such ethical dilemmas.[1] This guide will be informed by ethical theories and aims to shed light on what the accountancy profession can realistically be expected to contribute to improving the ethical climate of business.

When whistleblowing is placed in the broader context of accounting ethics it becomes clear that the profession tends to define ethics quite narrowly. Jack Maurice, writing as Secretary of the Chartered Accountants Joint Ethics Committee (CAJEC),[2] underlines this point as follows:

> To understand the ethics of the accountancy profession in the United Kingdom – or, for that matter, anywhere else in the developed nations of the world – a general acquaintance with the profession itself, and in particular the practising element in the profession, is more important than an appreciation of ethical theory. ... A second contention, or warning is that an understanding of the ethics of any established profession, even of the 'commercial' professions of law and accountancy, is unlikely to be achieved by an approach based on a study of 'business ethics'. (Maurice, 1996)

His doubts about the value of ethical theory in general, or business ethics in particular, arise from the specific and finite rules of these professions which are enforced upon their members by their professional bodies, rather than being more speculative and open-ended ethical requirements left to the conscience of the market or, more rarely, the sanction of the courts. Thus the previous chapter in this book (on 'Whistleblowing and Business Ethics') would not, on this view, be deemed an appropriate basis for considering the 'commercial' professions like accountancy.

As the majority of the members of the UK accountancy profession are not in professional practice, Maurice believes that the existence of 'these individual professional centres of excellence within the broader corporate governance of UK organisations *should* contribute, progressively, to a rise in those ethical standards which may be shared between professional and non-professional'. So the claim is being made that the narrower approach to ethics, 'enforced' by the profession, should produce better ethical results than a broader approach, reliant on a more voluntaristic understanding of ethics. This chapter will allow the reader to decide whether this view is right or whether it is an underlying reason why the profession is challenged by its critics, i.e. because it sets its own rules on a higher plain than ethical theory in general.

The dichotomy between narrower and broader definitions of accounting ethics has not gone unnoticed by the academic community. An important study, edited by Gowthorpe and Blake (1998), focuses on the limited attention given to the ethical aspects of accounting in the UK. They accept that, in a sense, Maurice's narrow definition is quite reasonable, in that few accountants are involved in making policy choices at the 'macro' level of setting accounting standards. However, they also emphasize the involvement of accountants at the level of individual firms or audits and the importance of understanding the ethical implications of the choices made by others. The accountant as whistle-blower is just one such possibility.

The view taken by some practitioners, that no moral involvement is needed beyond subscribing to the profession's ethical code, may be the practical consequence of rejecting the broader definition of accounting ethics. The reader should at least be aware of an alternative viewpoint, namely, that accountancy has a role in transforming the world through public understanding of economic realities. If this is the case, accounting choices become moral choices (Gowthorpe and Blake, 1998; Lehman, 1995). In any event, accountants may not be able to escape from moral dilemmas in their work which test the adequacy of their codes of conduct. The issue of whistleblowing brings this point out clearly.

The subject of whistleblowing and accountancy cannot be adequately addressed outside of the context of accounting ethics, whether narrowly or broadly defined. To allow the reader to assess their merits, a brief summary of the three main ethical theories will be provided. These conceptual frameworks, together with relevant provisions of the codes of conduct adopted by the professional bodies can then be deployed to examine the problems accountants face when performing their duties.

ETHICAL THEORIES

A book on accounting ethics in the USA by Cottell and Perlin (1990) discussed the two main ethical theories: utilitarianism and deontology.[3] There is also a third, which was not mentioned explicitly, called motivational ethical theory. Utilitarianism examines the *consequences* of actions in order to decide what is morally justified. It does this by attempting to maximize the good over the harmful consequences in order to secure the best long-term interests of the greatest number of people. Whistleblowers who act on this theory would take into account the likely consequences of their decisions for all concerned and only 'blow the whistle' if the benefits outweigh the costs. They would not take rules or duties into account in arriving at their decisions unless they are 'rule utilitarians'. In which case the rule to whistleblow, however defined, would only be applied if to do so would be expected to result in the maximum good. Critics of this theory might argue that it can apparently justify the imposition of a great deal of suffering on the whistleblower (and, perhaps, some others) provided many people benefit. There is also the practical difficulty of defining the likely benefits of whistleblowing.

Deontological theory maintains that right action is independent of consequences because there are rules and principles which are essentially right and should never be infringed. Thus a moral person would have a duty to whistleblow irrespective of the personal consequences, if the rules determining when it were right to do so had been met. The most influential deontological theory is derived from Immanuel Kant (1724–1804), although it is worth noting that originally this could be classed as a motivational ethical theory since he held that the rightness or wrongness of an act depended on the intentions behind it. However, it is justified to put Kantianism, in its various forms, under the category of deontology because motives became converted into duties, for example, through the application of the 'categorical imperative'. By this Kant meant that individuals should take actions, and only those actions, which they would want everyone to take in all circumstances, regardless of the consequences. More recent modifications of Kantian ethical theory have introduced greater flexibility. They address the criticisms of the categorical imperative that strict application can lead to disproportionate suffering – such as to the whistleblower where the likely costs can far outweigh the benefits – but at the price of partially undermining the notion that ethical conduct can be decided without reference to consequences.

Cottell and Perlin also referred to 'ethical realism' as an attempt to resolve the conflicts between utlitarianism and deontologism. However,it is interesting to note that both theories can lead to the same conclusion. The significance of ethical realism here lies in the role of 'intellectual authorities' within accounting communities in modifying or changing attitudes in their profession towards particular ethical principles. Later, we will see how this is happening in the UK with respect to whistleblowing, related in part to the Public Interest Disclosure Act 1998 (PIDA 1998).

There can be little doubt that both consequentialist ethical theory (utlitarianism) and ethical theory based on duties (deontology) can be relevant to resolving ethical conflicts faced by accountants. However, neither theory is necessarily adequate on its own and both may need to be considered in relation to motivational ethical theory. This requires us to ask questions about the underlying intentions of the professional bodies, or individual trainee and practising accountants, with respect to the issue of whistleblowing.[4]

Having identified the main ethical frameworks we will now apply them to the issues faced by different groups of accounting professionals.

ACCOUNTANTS EMPLOYED WITHIN ORGANIZATIONS

MANAGEMENT ACCOUNTANTS

The author sent letters to the five British accountancy bodies[5] requesting information on their latest policy positions on the subject of whistleblowing. Additionally, information on case histories was requested. Only the Chartered Institute of Management Accountants (CIMA) offered a substantive response and active assistance so their position is considered first.

CIMA's 'Ethical Guidelines' were approved by its Council in March 1992. In the Introduction to these Guidelines CIMA, in common with other professions, accepts its responsibility to the public:

> The accounting profession's public consists of employers, creditors, clients, governments, employees, investors, the business and financial community and others who rely on the *objectivity* and integrity of professional accountants to maintain the orderly functioning of commerce. This reliance imposes a public interest responsibility on the accountancy profession. The public interest is defined as the collective well-being of the community of people and institutions the professional accountant serves (Paragraph 7). [Emphasis in the original.]

The objectives of the accountancy profession are defined as being

> to work to the highest standards of professionalism, to attain the highest levels of performance and generally to meet the public interest requirement (Paragraph 11).

These objectives are to be met by four basic needs: credibility; professionalism; quality of services; and confidence. Professional accountants have, therefore, to observe the 'fundamental principles' contained in paragraph 13, namely

- Integrity
- Objectivity
- Professional Competence and Due Care
- Confidentiality

- Professional Behaviour
- Technical Standards

Part A of the 'Guidelines' applies to all CIMA members, including section 2 on the 'Resolution of Ethical Conflicts'. Members are expected to deal with 'identified and significant ethical issues in an employed situation' (paragraph 2.3) through the grievance procedure or such like of an organization and follow these wherever possible. If this does not resolve the problem, then the 'Guidelines' set out the further steps to be taken internally. Discussion of the issues involved and possible courses of action are permitted with an objective adviser or the member's professional accountancy body, provided no breach of the duty of confidentiality to the other parties occurs.

> If the ethical conflict still exists after fully exhausting all levels of internal review, the member as a last resort may have no other recourse on significant matters (e.g. fraud) than to resign and submit an information memorandum to an appropriate representative of his or her employing organisation (Paragraph 2.3).[6]

While external whistleblowing is not explicitly mentioned in the 'Guidelines' it would appear to be implicitly rejected here:

> Except when seeking advice from the Secretary of the Institute or when legally required to do so communication of information regarding the matter [i.e. ethical conflict] to persons outside the employing organisation is not considered appropriate (Paragraph 2.7).

Section 4 makes clear that the obligation not to make unauthorized disclosures to other persons of confidential information about an employer's affairs '...does not apply to disclosure of such information in order properly to discharge the individual's responsibility according to the profession's standards' (Paragraph 4.5). This is spelled out more positively in a subsequent paragraph: 'When there is a professional duty or right to disclose: i. to comply with technical standards and ethical requirements; such disclosure is not contrary to this section' (Paragraph 4.8.c).

The enactment of PIDA 1998 is welcomed by CIMA's Head of

Professional Standards, Mark Hayward, as a major advance in changing the 'cover-up' culture. Nevertheless, he emphasizes the need for any employee who wants to 'blow the whistle' to think very carefully and be sure of their ground. As regards external whistleblowing, he emphasizes that PIDA 1998 only offers protection under certain conditions (see chapter 2).[7]

A comparison between the UK and USA in relation to ethics in management accountancy was undertaken by Cashmore (1994). On the 'Resolution of Ethical Conflicts', she discovered that the Institute of Management Accountants (IMA) in the USA was offering almost identical advice to that given by CIMA. However, the American Institute of Certified Public Accountants (AICPA) restructured its Code of Professional Conduct in 1988 to bring under its more wide-ranging guidelines almost half of all Certified Public Accountants employed as management accountants. This revision was intended 'to shift the emphasis away from a rule-oriented code towards a code which placed greater reliance on ethical principles'(Shaub and Brown, 1994). Unlike the CIMA principles and IMA standards, the AICPA 'Principles of Professional Conduct' include the public interest.

The practical difficulty of being both loyal to 'the management team' and yet placing the public interest first has led some to 'blow the whistle'. However, even in the USA, many management accountants still view whistleblowing as a sign of disloyalty. Consequently Shaub and Brown (1994) recommend the creation of an atmosphere of cooperation among professionals, through management accountants reporting their concerns to auditors who may, in turn, report them to the audit committee. What both Shaub and Brown, on the one hand, and Cashmore, on the other hand, agree on is that for the management accountant simply to resign is no solution. First, this punishes the person who has acted with integrity. Second, and more importantly, it represents a failure on that person's part to uphold the public interest because malpractice is likely to continue. Even the use of financial rewards in the USA (see below) may not offer sufficient monetary compensation for blighted career prospects.

ASSESSMENT

The application of a broader definition of accounting ethics, based on general ethical theories, may favour public interest over commercial confidentiality when malpractice has been identified by management accountants in their employing organization. This can result in intense suffering for those who decide to 'blow the whistle'. Hence the narrower definition of accounting ethics applied by professional bodies may be preferred because it tends to put commercial confidentiality above public interest and so avoids external whistleblowing.

PIDA 1998 has enabled CIMA to modify its previous (implicit) stance on external whistleblowing while remaining cautious because of the risks involved – an example of 'ethical realism' discussed earlier. Thus paragraph 2.7 of Part A of its 'Guidelines' needs amending in order to reflect the new situation. However,there are no signs of any move away from 'rule-based ethics' comparable to the steps taken by the AICPA, which would require members to exercise more of their own ethical judgement. While some may criticize this, the case studies below help to illustrate the difficulties involved.

Case Study (1) MIS Limited
(by Richardson and Richardson in Gowthorpe and Blake, 1998)
This UK company was owned and managed by Philip, its sole director. It had a turnover of £2.5 million and was heavily dependent on a bank overdraft facility to cope with an on-going liquidity problem arising from his personal lifestyle. MIS Ltd had its base in the north Midlands where a very small staff maintained its administration and looked after its employees at clients' sites around the world.

A new management accountant was recruited by Philip to help him provide more timely and regular information for the bank. However, the new systems she introduced had the effect of highlighting the poor quality of Philip's decision-making. Likewise the cash flow forecasts and tighter controls on liquidity revealed the impact of Philip's continuous cash drawings from company funds for his personal use. After the company overdraft facility was repeatedly breached the bank intervened and for a time this introduced a powerful controlling influence on Philip. However, this influence receded when the company's financial position improved. Philip's personal spending rose again until a crisis was precipitated by his decision to buy a new £200,000 house, using company funds of £40,000 to finance the deposit and other expenses for this 'southern office'. The company was unable to meet its VAT commitments and became the subject of official investigations. Subsequently it failed.

ASSESSMENT

Richardson *et al.* offer an analysis of the accountant's reflections on her position at MIS Ltd in this real-life case study. Her options were: to resign from the company; to whistleblow to the bank or Inland Revenue or someone else who could affect Philip's behaviour; or to try again to use persuasive tactics on her boss. The accountant's own personal situation held her back from the first two options. While she was sure Philip's behaviour was unethical, she was aware this might be her personal value system rather than a more general societal perspective. She was unsure whether Philip's behaviour was illegal. Despite being a student member of a professional body of accountants studying related subjects part-time at a local university she did not know how much assistance might be available and did not make enquiries from either institution.

In deciding whether or not to whistleblow (her 'least-favoured option'), she considered the position of stakeholders. The bank was well secured but she was uncomfortable negotiating time extensions with the Inland Revenue and Customs and Excise when she knew the precarious position of the company and the underlying cause. Her greatest concern was for the less powerful stakeholders, for example, employees and subcontractors. Whistleblowing, even on an informal basis, would have increased the risks of the company folding. She could not know, in advance, that it would fail and kept hoping, despite a growing conviction that Philip could not change his behaviour, that he would. Yet her efforts to bring this change about were muted because of her fear that he would react very adversely.

A comparison can be made with the collapse of the Bank of Credit and Commerce International (BCCI), where Vivian Ambrose of the UK regional inspection department decided to blow the whistle. He wrote to Tony Benn MP 'alleging widespread corruption and nepotism and "apparent incompetence by executives"' (Vinten, October 1992). Unfortunately the letter which Tony Benn forwarded to two government departments was lost. The situations in MIS Ltd and BCCI were different. However, they raise the important question as to whether early whistleblowing might save rather than cost jobs.

The dilemma of whether or not to whistleblow was summarized by Richardson as follows:

> On the one hand the accountant perceived a clear duty to act in the public interest and she considered the behaviour of her boss to be of such unfair, immoral, improper, perhaps illegal proportions that she was almost honour-bound to bring it to the attention of 'someone with power'. Paradoxically, she was also aware that accountants, more than any other type of employee, have a duty of confidentiality and should not be tainted by any collusion in improper or illegal acts. (Richardson and Richardson, 1998)

Likewise (from a consequentialist perspective) the desire to whistleblow was stimulated by the fear of allowing questionable practices to go unchecked to the point where her active collusion might be imputed. On the other hand, there was the fear that if the point of connivance had already been passed (she didn't think so) then whistleblowing would have been more difficult. The possibility of discussing her concerns with the most recently appointed auditor was lost when he resigned without making contact with her. In the event, she tendered her resignation before the company folded but did not offer the real reason for leaving.

The reader is recommended to study this case in depth by referring to the original source and attempting to apply both professional codes of conduct and general theories of ethics discussed earlier in this chapter. It is worth considering what difference, if any, the PIDA 1998 might have made to the accountant's decision not to whistleblow.

Case Study (2) ZAP Company
(by Cottell and Perlin, 1990)
ZAP is a high-technology, multinational corporation and one of the top fifty American organizations. A ZAP factory in a certain city manufactures copper wiring using older plant that every day flushes twice the maximum permitted amount of effluent into the municipal sewage system. Copper is a poisonous substance for

water animals but not usually for human beings. Joe Storms, a cost accountant at the plant, learns about these infringements of the city's regulations and the consequent environmental dangers. Because his immediate supervisors ignore his concerns, he speaks to the plant manager, Mr Clyde. He urges Joe not to make waves because:(1) the plant will shortly be sold to another company; (2) ZAP plans to build a new factory with the latest anti-pollution equipment; and (3) no city inspector has served notice of any copper pollution. Within two years ZAP would be out of the city. However, Joe remains very concerned and his anxieties are not alleviated when the corporation hires a new public relations firm to promote itself as 'citizens concerned about the environment'.

ASSESSMENT

Cottell and Perlin suggest that Joe has a difficult range of choices on whistleblowing: he can do nothing; he could appeal to higher management within ZAP; he might warn Mr Clyde that unless plans are quickly made to limit effluent from the plant he will 'go public'; or he could call a press conference and tell the world that ZAP is a major pollutor. Having distinguished the ethical viewpoints of the various parties and identified the main value conflicts, Cottell and Perlin apply the utilitarian and deontological approaches and ethical realism in order to find an ethically justifiable course of action. Interestingly, they do not try to apply any specific professional code of conduct,although they point out that if Joe were a member of the National Association of Accountants he might get help from his local chapter.

The conclusion Cottell and Perlin reach is that 'a principled approach to the ZAP Company dilemma *seems* to lead in the direction of whistleblowing' (emphasis in the original). However, this is heavily qualified by the need to protect Joe from reprisals (which may not be possible). Cottell and Perlin go on to point out that were Joe to remain silent he would be infringing various principles: by acting in self-interest or, by reason of loyalty to his firm, for the benefit of those engaged in malpractice. Thus, from a utilitarian viewpoint, it can also be asked whether society or individual companies would benefit in a system that allowed rampant pollution and protected law-breakers? Cottell and Perlin conclude that

If we support whistleblowers, *we may be stating that we as a profession believe that public values predominate over narrow corporate needs*. If we defend principled whistleblowers (like Joe) as a matter of policy, we proclaim our concern for the less powerful in an immense bureaucracy. We may even provide a check to bureaucratic power. These are ethical matters of far-reaching significance (emphasis added).

Again the reader is recommended to the original source and may wish to contrast Cottell and Perlin's assessment with one based on a professional code of conduct.

FINANCIAL ACCOUNTANTS

Much of the previous section will apply to other categories of accountant, particularly as virtually all 110 member bodies of the International Federation of Accountants subscribe to similar ethical guidelines (Maurice, 1996). Some additional points can be made, though, in relation to whistleblowing and cases cited to illustrate differences of context and emphasis.

A study by Likierman and Taylor for the members of the Chartered Association of Certified Accountants (ACCA) in 1990 offered guidance to accountants in industry and commerce on a range of issues arising from the 'broader' definition of ethics. As far as unauthorized disclosures of information were concerned, arising from an ethical dilemma, their advice was very clear:

Whistleblowing involves a breach of trust by an employee and cannot therefore be justified on a strict interpretation of what constitutes *proper professional conduct* (emphasis in the original).

The course of action ACCA members were expected to follow was similar to that outlined for CIMA above, i.e. internal discussion of the matter through successive levels of management or other relevant authority and, if the matter was still unresolved, a member might have to resign, 'putting the matter in writing for the record'. However, Likierman and Taylor recognized the difficulty where resignation might not be a sufficient remedy and where there was criminal action by directors. The 'public disclosure might be justified in the public interest' but the courts had not defined 'public interest' and (at that time) a member was not offered legal protection. Moreover, the authors pointed out the lack of regard for whistleblowers as far as existing employees or future employers were concerned.

However, whistleblowing is countenanced between one accountant and another. The members of the Institute of Chartered Accountants in England and Wales (ICAEW) have approved a rule which obliges chartered accountants to 'blow the whistle' on colleagues who perform dishonest or bad work. This move was undertaken as part of the Institute's reshaping of its disciplinary procedures (Vinten, 1999).

ACCOUNTANTS IN THE PUBLIC SECTOR

A working paper by Gerald Vinten was published in 1993 which considered the views of 83 public sector accountant members of ACCA. The advice given by Likierman and Taylor on whistleblowing was repeated, with minor modifications. However, in addition, a positive view and detailed guidance was offered on setting up codes of practice for whistleblowing.

Case Study: US Department of Transportation
A true-life situation involving an architect who blew the whistle on alleged fraud and corruption in a state agency in 1988 is reported by Mintz (1997) in his book on accounting ethics. It is noteworthy for illustrating how even the use of the state's Whistleblower Act had not prevented the individual concerned from running into debts of $4.6 million for legal costs and being unemployed for four years at the time of writing. This was despite her successful lawsuits against the state.

ACCOUNTANTS IN PROFESSIONAL PRACTICE

The difficulties for accountants in professional practice, especially as auditors, in countenancing any form of whistleblowing (i.e. unauthorized disclosure) are even greater, because such breaches of client confidentiality would tend to undermine the business community's confidence in the profession itself. Significantly, although the PIDA 1998 in the UK extends the meaning of 'worker' beyond much existing employment law, it still specifically excludes those who provide services in a professional–client or business–client relationship.

The US position illustrates the conflicts of interest. A critique of the AICPA Code of Professional Conduct, which it may be recalled puts primary emphasis on the accountant's responsibility to the public (Article II), stressed that the requirements of the Code on confidential client information (Rule 301) prevented the accountant from publicly disclosing such information without the client's specific consent (Collins and Schultz, 1995). The authors argued that enforcement of Rule 301, while perhaps strengthening relations between accountants and their clients, could hardly be described as in the public interest if the public was harmed because a client firm's activities could not be discussed under that Rule.

ACCOUNTANTS AS AUDITORS

Only a few major studies have been done on whistleblowing and auditors (Vinten, 1992; Chambers, 1995). Professor Chambers's personal views, as a director of the Institute of Internal Auditors, are especially interesting on where responsibility to act lies when there is evidence of wrongdoing. An internal auditor in a business position which fails to come up to the Institute's recommendations may not have to resign but should try to persuade management to improve matters. He or she must act professionally and seek to preserve client confidentiality:

Having clearly and exhaustively reported matters of concern relating to wrongdoing to those to whom the auditor is authorised to report, the auditor has discharged his or her professional responsibilities. The auditor has no authority to compel management to respond, nor to initiate corrective action on the auditor's own authority. The auditor is an advisor only – not an executive, except with respect to managing the audit function itself. *So those to whom internal audit has reported (which are likely to be line management and should also be the Board) have the total responsibility for not actioning audit findings and recommendations satisfactorily. This means that they are also responsible for failure to remedy a reported wrongdoing* (emphasis added).

This matter of where responsibility to act lies is a very important but often neglected aspect of whistleblowing. Chambers goes on to consider whether an internal auditor should *ever* 'blow the whistle' externally without management approval or legal and industrial regulation. He suggests that while there is never a *professional* obligation to whistleblow, there may be a *personal duty* in relation to wider considerations of morality, if not professional ethics.[8] In his view the dilemma would be resolved by whistle-blowers' protection legislation.

Indeed, Section 43F of the Employment Rights Act 1996 (ERA 1996) protects workers who make qualifying disclosures in good faith to such bodies as the Financial Services Authority and other regulatory authorities, provided the worker reasonably believes the matter falls within the remit of the prescribed person and that the information and any allegation contained in it are substantially true. Where a regulator has been 'prescribed' there is no require-ment that the specific disclosure be reasonable, nor that the malpractice be serious nor even that the matter be raised internally first. However, the standard of evidence is higher than in the case of internal whistleblowing (see also Hayes, 1996).[9] Consequently, Section 43F ERA 1996 may ease the internal auditor's burden but 'blowing the whistle' is still likely to go very much against the grain of professionalism.

CONCLUSION

In a sense Chambers provides a helpful peg on which to hang some concluding comments. While recognizing the need for professionals to abide by a code of ethics and respect client confi-dentiality, he also acknowledges a broader ethical obligation to society which may necessitate whistleblowing. However, no law could ever, on its own, resolve this ethical dilemma since legisla-tion could not be drafted that would cover every circumstance in which such dilemmas might arise.

It may be no coincidence that the narrower definition of accounting ethics is espoused mainly by accountants in business or in practice, while the broader definition is often preferred by accountants in academia. The former face the realities of the market economy; the latter less so. That professional accountancy bodies put client confidentiality above the public interest, simply reflects the normal self-interest of any professional body and its members. If they eschew a broader definition of accounting ethics it may be because the application of such ethical frameworks throws light on that self-interest and suggests instead a selflessness which a few isolated whistleblowers may have. Academic accountants are right to draw attention to the deficiencies of codes of ethics and the need for a broader definition but should not expect what neither professional bodies nor the law alone can deliver to protect whistleblowers.

Perhaps the right balance to strike in accounting ethics is brought out by the issue of whistleblowing. The professional accountancy bodies need to develop specific guidelines for resolving ethical conflicts faced by their members at work but they might also encourage those members to apply broader definitions of ethics in relation to their personal obligations to society. The ethical dilemmas demonstrated by the few in-depth case studies we have on whistleblowing accountants may reveal why the focus on codes of ethics cannot by itself be expected to raise standards more generally in business and may sometimes fail even to adequately address conflicts of interest. Yet no one should expect a single issue, albeit an important one like whistleblowing, to become the basis for resolving all the problems of greed and corruption in society. A start has been made in changing the culture of 'cover-up' and accountants could have a pivotal role in taking this forward, but to tackle the underlying causes of whistleblowing is beyond their power to achieve alone.

ACKNOWLEDGEMENT

The author gratefully acknowledges the assistance of the Secretary and other officers of the Chartered Institute of Management Accountants while undertaking the research for this chapter. However, the responsibility for any errors and omissions remains the author's alone.

BIBLIOGRAPHY

Beach, J.E. (1984) 'Code of ethics: the professional catch 22', *Journal of Accounting and Public Policy*, pp. 311–23.

Cashmore, C. (1994) 'Some preliminary considerations on ethics in management accountancy', London Guildhall University Occasional Paper.

Chambers, Andrew (1995) 'Whistleblowing and the internal auditor', *Business Ethics: A European Review*, October, pp. 192–8.

Chartered Institute of Management Accountants (March 1992) 'Ethical Guidelines', London, CIMA.

Collins, Allison, and Schultz,Norm (1995) 'A critical examination of the AICPA Code of Professional Conduct', *Journal of Business Ethics*, pp. 31–41.

Cottell, Philip G., and Perlin, Terry M. (1990) *Accounting Ethics: A Practical Guide for Professionals*, Westport, Connecticut, Quorum Books.

Gowthorpe, Catherine and Blake,John (eds) (1998) *Ethical Issues in Accounting*, London, Routledge.

Hayes, Edward (1996) 'Whistleblowing in the dark', *Accountancy*, June, p. 125.

Hearn, Sam (1999) 'Whistleblowing: implementing an employee hotline', *Management Accounting*, February, pp. 35–6.

Lehman, Cheryl R. (1995) *Accounting's Changing Role in Social Conflict*, London, Paul Chapman.

Likierman, Andrew and Taylor, Alison (1990) *Ethics and Accountants in Industry and Commerce: Potential Problems and Existing Guidance*, London, Chartered Association of Certified Accountants.

Loeb, Stephen E. and Rockness, Joanne (1992) 'Accounting ethics and education: a response', *Journal of Business Ethics*, pp. 485–90.

Maurice, Jack (1996) *Accounting Ethics*, London, Pitman.

Mintz, Steven M. (1997) *Cases in Accounting Ethics and Professionalism*, New York, McGraw Hill.

Richardson, Susan, and Richardson, Bill (1998) 'The accountant as whistleblower', in Gowthorpe, Catherine and Blake, John (eds), *Ethical Issues in Accounting*, London, Routledge, pp. 41–62.

Shaub, Michael K., and Brown,James (1994) 'Whistleblowing management accountants: a US view', in Vinten,Gerald (ed.), *Whistleblowing: Subversion or Corporate Citizenship?*, London, Paul Chapman, pp. 106–17.

Vinten, Gerald (October 1992) 'Whistleblowing auditors – the ultimate oxymoron?', *Business Ethics: A European Review*, pp. 248–55.

Vinten, Gerald (1992) 'Whistleblowing auditors: a contradiction in terms?', Occasional Research Paper No. 12; ACCA Technical and Research Committee, London.

Vinten, Gerald (1993) 'Towards a code of ethics for accountants in the public sector', City University Business School Working Paper, London.

Vinten, Gerald (1999) 'Whistleblowing UK style', Southampton Business School Discussion Paper.

NOTES

1. It should be noted, though, that the literature review is largely restricted to the United Kingdom and United States of America.
2. The CAJEC consists of the Institute of Chartered Accountants in England and Wales (ICAEW), the Institute of Chartered Accountants of Scotland (ICAS)

and the Institute of Chartered Accountants in Ireland (ICAI). Maurice notes that the Chartered Association of Certified Accountants (ACCA) has similar ethical requirements in most respects to those of 'the three'.

3. I have adapted their frameworks to apply to whistleblowing.
4. The religious beliefs of individual accountants may be relevant here.
5. Letters dated 15 July 1999 were sent to the Chief Executive or Secretary of ICAEW, ICAS, ACCA, the Chartered Institute of Management Accountants (CIMA) and the Chartered Institute of Public Finance and Accountancy (CIPFA).
6. See also para. 2.5.
7. CIMA Press Release, 2 July 1999.
8. In this connection the whistleblower, Paul van Buitenen, then an internal auditor who played a significant part in the fall of the European Commission would provide an interesting case study. Suspended from his job in December 1998 after 'leaking' information to the European Parliament on alleged fraud and mismanagement in the EC, he was reported to have received 'only' a formal reprimand (*Financial Times*, 5 October 1999).
9. Edward Hayes reports on the Pensions Act 1995 which obliges auditors of pension schemes to provide a written report to the Occupational Pensions Regulatory Authority of any irregularities in the administering of the schemes.

5

Whistleblowing and Human Resource Management

DAVID LEWIS AND MALCOLM SARGEANT

Although many employers have mission statements which refer to the need for high standards of ethical behaviour, until recently whistleblowing codes were rarely used as a method of achieving this goal. In this chapter we examine the reasons for producing whistleblowing policies and procedures and make practical proposals about their possible contents and operation.

WHY HAVE A WHISTLEBLOWING CODE?

In the USA, the Organizational Sentencing Guidelines have focused attention on the extent to which employers have developed self-governance systems that address whistleblowers' concerns. To take advantage of these Guidelines employers must adopt mechanisms to promote internal reporting and to facilitate remedial action in the event that concerns prove well founded. In chapter 2 we saw that the Public Interest Disclosure Act 1998 (PIDA 1998) does not oblige UK employers to have whistleblowing procedures but provides obvious benefits to those who do have them. According to Public Concern at Work (PCAW), 'unless there are effective procedures in place which demonstrate your organisation's willingness to listen and address concerns, employees are more likely to take their concerns outside – and to be protected by the Act in doing so. Employers with good whistleblowing policies and procedures are less likely to be exposed to claims under the Act. Additionally, it is less likely that any wider public disclosure will be protected under the Act.'[1]

The responsibility for creating an open and communicative culture rests with top management. In practice many organizations will give the personnel or human resources department the task of devising a whistleblowing procedure and ensuring that it

fits in with other procedures.[2] Indeed, unless careful consideration is given to the potential impact of whistleblowing on discipline (see below, page 62), there may be a suspicion that a new
procedure could be used to monitor performance and investigate
staff without their knowledge. If everyone in the organization is
to understand why a whistleblowing procedure is being introduced and what it is trying to achieve, it is vital to get the
commitment of both senior management and worker representatives.[3] Ideally there should be agreement as to the contents of a
whistleblowing code which contains both a policy statement and
a procedure.

The following arguments might be used in order to persuade
senior management of the desirability of formulating such a Code:

- by deterring malpractice and avoiding crisis management it can
  contribute to the efficient running of the organization
- by providing accountability it can help to maintain the organization's reputation
- it can help to ensure compliance with the law and minimize
  external disclosures
- it is a good practice which does not cost much to implement

A survey of 57 private and 57 public-sector organizations
conducted by Industrial Relations Services Employment Trends
and Public Concern at Work in May 1999 (henceforward the
IRS/PCAW survey) found that 46 organizations had, and 44
intended to introduce shortly, a whistleblowing policy.[4] Public-
sector employers were more more likely than those in the private
sector to have a policy or have plans – 95 per cent compared with
63 per cent in the private sector. Respondents were asked to indicate from a given list what provided the impetus to introduce a
whistleblowing policy. Several employers offered more than one
reason but the motives behind the introduction of such policies
were the same within both the public and private sector. The
reasons identified were: good practice (60 employers); to comply
with the law (38 employers); because management saw it as an
issue (20 employers); requested by a union (6 employers) and
because an incident highlighted the need for a policy (2 employers).

FORMULATING A WHISTLEBLOWING POLICY

Before considering the issues involved in devising an appropriate whistleblowing *procedure*, we turn first to the possible contents of a whistleblowing *policy*. In order to reflect the Nolan Committee's views on best practice in this area,it is suggested that such a policy might contain the following:

- a clear statement that malpractice is taken seriously in the organization and an indication of the sorts of matters regarded as malpractice
- respect for the confidentiality of staff raising concerns if they wish, and the opportunity to raise concerns outside the line-management structure
- penalties for making false and malicious allegations
- an indication of the proper way in which concerns may be raised outside the organization if necessary.[5]

According to the Institute of Management Foundation's 'Action checklist', 'To be effective there should be a sense of organizational ownership of a whistleblowing policy. Discuss the issues at the beginning, explaining the reasons behind the policy and dealing with objections and worries. Circulate the draft policy to employees or make it available for comments and suggestions.'[6] In the authors' opinion, a policy statement is likely to be more influential if it has been agreed with or discussed by relevant trade unions (or other workers' representatives) and has their support. Trade unions have always had an important role as a watchdog and have supported members who 'speak up'. They are likely to be keen to be involved, particularly if they can negotiate over both the contents of the procedure and how problems which it highlights can be resolved. Indeed, some unions will have firm ideas about how they would like such procedures to operate (see chapter 9). Reflecting the fact that trade unions are more likely to be recognized by public-sector than private-sector employers, 34 public-sector employers in the IRS/PCAW survey involved a trade union representative in formulating a whistleblowing policy compared with 8 private-sector organizations. Indeed, 3 public sector respondents negotiated the introduction of their policies.

WHO AND WHAT SHOULD BE COVERED BY A PROCEDURE?

Perhaps the first matter to be addressed in relation to a whistle-blowing procedure is its scope – to whom does it apply and what issues does it cover? Given the broad definition of a worker contained in Section 43K (1) of the Employment Rights Act 1996 (see chapter 2), a procedure should apply not only to employees but should also extend to contractors and other suppliers of services.

As regards coverage of issues, a whistleblowing procedure does not replace existing procedures, for example, those for handling grievances or equal opportunity matters. Thus it should be made clear that the whistleblowing procedure is intended to be used only where a concern falls outside the scope of other procedures. According to the Institute of Personnel and Development: 'It is preferable to deal with whistleblowing separately, rather than as an extension to or part of an existing procedure, while cross-referencing procedures on discipline and grievances. This is mainly because the scale of risk to the organization and to the employee will generally be significantly greater in whistleblowing cases than with other matters. In addition, the whistleblower may have no grievance in relation to terms and conditions, or indeed in relation to the employer (his or her concern may for example relate to the conduct of a contractor).'[7]

A procedure should obviously allow concerns to be raised about the following matters because they are treated by Section 43B(1) Employment Rights Act 1996 as 'qualifying disclosures' (see chapter 2): a criminal offence; a failure to comply with any legal obligation; danger to the health and safety of any individual; damage to the environment; and the deliberate concealment of information tending to show any of the matters listed above. However, the organization may wish to go further by inviting people to report concerns about other unethical conduct.[8] If that is the case, it is obviously imperative to ensure that the contents of any code of conduct or ethics are also well understood.

CONFIDENTIALITY AND ANONYMITY

The next issue to be considered is that of safeguards. A whistle-blowing procedure should assure potential users that, whenever possible, the organization will protect the identity of those who raise a concern and do not want their name disclosed. However, it must also be pointed out that the investigation of a concern may occasionally reveal the source of information. In addition, the organization may require a statement by the person reporting the concern as part of the process of collecting evidence. Employers tend to discourage anonymous reporting on the grounds that it is often not very helpful and might suggest that the discloser is doing something morally wrong. Nevertheless, an organization might wish to reserve the right to consider concerns which are raised anonymously. In exercising any discretion the factors to be taken into account might include the seriousness of the issues raised and the likelihood of obtaining information from attributable sources.

In a survey of local authorities (henceforward the local authority survey), 28 of the 39 councils who had a whistleblowing procedure stated that requests for confidentiality would be respected and 24 allowed concerns to be raised anonymously.[9] In an earlier survey of *The Times* Top 500 UK Firms (henceforward the *Top 500* survey), 10 of the 11 organizations with a written procedure indicated that they allowed employees to preserve their anonymity.[10] Since both these pieces of research revealed a trend towards the introduction of 'hotlines', a specific survey was conducted in 1998 on this method of reporting concerns (henceforward the 'hotline' survey).[11] All 14 respondents gave undertakings about maintaining confidentiality and half gave this in writing. Two organizations did not indicate whether or not information supplied by anonymous callers would be accepted. However, 11 of the remaining 12 respondents said that such information would be recorded. In the IRS/PCAW survey, two-thirds of employers indicated that their whistleblowing policy offered confidentiality to users. Information supplied anonymously was recorded by 56 of the 90 respondents.

DEALING WITH REPRISALS AND MALICIOUS ALLEGATIONS

Perhaps the best way of acknowledging the perceived vulnerability of whistleblowers would be to give undertakings about possible reprisals. The Public Interest Disclosure Act 1998 provides legal remedies both to those who are dismissed or are subjected to a detriment for making a protected disclosure (see pages 19–20). A whistleblowing procedure should therefore include an unequivocal statement to the effect that the employer will not tolerate any harassment or victimization (including informal pressures) and will take appropriate action in order to protect a person who has reasonable grounds for raising a concern. Thus disciplinary rules should state that victimization or deterring employees from raising legitimate concerns will constitute serious misconduct. Additional steps may have to be taken to ensure that non-employees are protected from reprisals. In the IRS/PCAW survey, less than a half of respondents (44) reported that victimization of a whistleblower would lead to disciplinary action. However, 63 per cent of respondents indicated that it was a disciplinary offence to destroy or conceal evidence of malpractice.

Employers should also make it clear that they will protect themselves and their staff from false and malicious expressions of concern by taking disciplinary action where appropriate. In the local authority survey, 41 per cent of authorities who had a procedure indicated that it provided for action to be taken against those who acted maliciously in relation to unfounded allegations. Of course, concerns which are genuinely believed may prove to be unfounded on investigation. Thus organizations should also undertake to ensure that the negative impact of either a malicious or unfounded allegation about any person is minimized. Of course,one way of protecting managers from disgruntled poor performers is by ensuring that performance reviews are properly documented.

OBTAINING ADVICE AND ASSISTANCE

It follows from what has been said already that a whistleblowing procedure should specifically encourage workers to seek advice at an early stage. It should indicate where advice can be obtained from internally, for example, from designated persons (see below). However,in recognition of the fact that some workers might insist on a more objective or independent opinion,it might also be sensible to inform staff about external sources, for example, Public Concern at Work's confidential helpline or persons prescribed by the Public Interest Disclosure (Prescribed Persons) Order 1999 (see page 18). In addition, workers should be informed that they have the right to be represented by their trade union, staff association or a friend when invoking the procedure.[12] In the IRS/PCAW survey, two-thirds of respondents stated that employees could bring a union representative or colleague with them to a meeting dealing with a concern. Just over a third of respondents (largely in the public sector) said that independent advice was available to whistleblowers.

WITH WHOM SHOULD A CONCERN BE RAISED?

Concerns should normally be raised initially with an appropriate level of line management, i.e. the immediate supervisor or his/her manager. However, the most appropriate person to contact will depend upon the seriousness and sensitivity of the issues involved and who is suspected of malpractice. Thus it is recommended that included in or attached to the procedure should be the names and work addresses of 'designated persons'. Such people will be those who have agreed to be a point of contact for workers wishing to report a concern but who do not want to approach their line manager initially. For example, departmental heads, the chief accountant or head of human resources might be appropriate to serve as 'designated persons'.

Under such a scheme line managers would report that a concern had been received by them to a 'designated person'. In some organizations 'hotlines' have been introduced as an alternative channel of communication (see page 61). Whether this operates internally or via an external provider, information about a concern should eventually reach a 'designated person' or the person in the organization who is ultimately responsible for ensuring concerns are investigated (see page 64 on 'responsible persons'). In the local authority survey, 19 (49 per cent) of the procedures suggested more than one person with whom concerns should be raised initially, and 25 authorities with a procedure (64 per cent) gave employees an option as to whom to approach if they continued to have concerns. In the IRS/PCAW survey, almost two-thirds of respondents had policies which indicated that an employee could raise a concern with someone other than their immediate line manager.

HOW SHOULD A CONCERN BE RAISED?

A whistleblowing procedure should give people the choice of raising their concerns verbally or in writing. Those willing to make a written report could be encouraged to use a particular format; ideally, one which has been agreed with trade union or other employee representatives. For example, giving relevant times and dates in describing the background to the concern and indicating why the worker is particularly worried about the situation. It should be made clear that, although whistleblowers are not expected to prove the truth of an allegation, it will be necessary to demonstrate to the person contacted that there are sufficient grounds for concern. It might also be pointed out that the earlier a concern is expressed the easier it might be to take remedial action.

HOW SHOULD A CONCERN BE HANDLED?

For the avoidance of doubt, it might be useful if the procedure states that the action to be taken by the organization will depend on the nature of the concern. An initial confidential interview should be conducted by the 'designated person' who should send an agreed summary or report of it to the person with overall responsibility for the whistleblowing procedure. This 'responsible person', who should be the Chief Executive or other senior person in the organization, should maintain a record of concerns raised and their outcomes for monitoring purposes (see below). In the IRS/PCAW survey,44 per cent of respondents stated that the director or chief executive had overall responsibility for the whistleblowing policy.

On the basis of the 'designated person's' summary or report, the 'responsible person' should decide whether or not an investigation is required and, if so, what form it should take. In the IRS/PCAW survey, 44 respondents followed a set procedure for investigating an allegation. 25 respondents indicated that the line manager was responsible for investigating concerns and 23 stated that the personnel function leads the investigation. Where a concern is about the 'responsible person', the 'designated person' should refer the matter to the chairperson of the organization (or equivalent) who will decide how to proceed and whether an external investigation is appropriate. Concerns or allegations which fall within the scope of other procedures, for example discrimination issues, should normally be referred for consideration under those procedures.

The whistleblowing procedure should point out that some concerns may be dealt with by agreed action without the need for investigation. Equally, sometimes, urgent action may be required before any investigation is conducted. In order to protect the confidentiality both of the person reporting and the subject of the concern, it should be provided that the person being investigated will not be informed until (or if) it becomes necessary to do so. It must also be pointed out that where there are serious allegations of misconduct a person under investigation may have to be suspended. If as a result of an investigation a prima facie case of misconduct is established, the organization's disciplinary rules and procedure will have to be invoked.

As with other employment procedures, it is good practice for a whistleblowing procedure to contain time limits for action to be taken. Thus, within a stipulated period after a concern has been raised, for example 10 working days, the 'designated person' should:

- send the whistleblower a copy of the initial interview summary which was sent to the 'responsible person'
- state how the organization proposes to deal with the matter and whether preliminary enquiries have been conducted
- indicate whether further investigations will take place and, if not, why not
- give an estimate as to how long it will take to provide a final response
- supply information about staff-support mechanisms, for example advice and counselling

The amount of contact between the whistleblower and those investigating the concern will depend on the nature of the concern, the potential difficulties involved and the clarity of the information that has been provided. The procedure should point out that, where necessary, further information may be sought from the whistleblower. Indeed, where very serious allegations are made it may be appropriate to hold a formal enquiry and/or refer the matter to the police. Whistleblowers should also be reminded that they have the right to be represented by trade union, staff association or friend at any stage.

In order to demonstrate the efficacy of the procedure (and avoid legitimate external disclosures) whistleblowers need to be assured that their concerns have been properly addressed. Thus the procedure should specify that the 'responsible person' will inform the 'designated person' as to the outcome of any investigation. In turn, the 'designated person' should arrange a meeting with the whistleblower in order to provide as much information as possible about the outcome of any investigation. Again,this feedback should be provided within agreed time limits. In the IRS/PCAW survey,more than two-thirds of respondents aimed to inform the whistleblower about the outcome of the investigation.

TAKING THE MATTER FURTHER

The whistleblowing procedure is intended to provide workers with an avenue to raise concerns within the organization. However, a person who is dissatisfied with the organization's response may wish to take the matter outside. Since workers have legal protection if they make external disclosures in certain circumstances (see chapter 2),it is in an employer's interest to specify who they regard as appropriate recipients. It is obviously desirable that any external scrutiny is conducted by a reputable body rather than the general media. Thus employers are advised to draw attention to the list of persons prescribed by Regulations, relevant professional bodies or agencies with specialist expertise,for example, Public Concern at Work. Although employers would prefer workers who take their concern outside the organization not to divulge confidential information, it should be noted that Section 43J ERA 1996 renders 'gagging clauses' ineffective in so far as they purport to inhibit a person from making a protected disclosure. In the IRS/PCAW survey, 58 respondents stated that if the whistleblower is dissatisfied with how their concern has been handled they can take it further.

COMMUNICATING AND MONITORING THE PROCEDURE

Workers can be made aware of the contents of a whistleblowing procedure by a variety of mechanisms, for example, induction training, posters, contracts of employment and newsletters. The *The Times* Top 500,the local authority and the IRS/PCAW surveys all revealed that the method most commonly used was the staff handbook. However,the report on local authorities suggests that the more personalized and diverse the ways the procedures were promoted,the more likely they were to be used. Ideally a flowchart or diagram should be supplied with the procedure which shows precisely how the organization will process a concern. According to the IRS/PCAW survey, training for managers about how the whistleblowing policy works was not common – only 18 respondents had instigated this and 12 were planning to do so. However, 24 respondents trained managers on what they should do if a concern was raised and a further 11 planned to offer such training. Issuing written guidance was the most common form of training.

As with other procedures, it would be sensible for employers to commit themselves to monitor and review the operation of the whistleblowing procedure on a regular basis. In the local authority survey, 21 of the councils with a procedure (54 per cent) stated that they had such arrangements. In the IRS/PCAW survey, 60 per cent of respondents indicated that they maintain records of how a concern is dealt with under their policy. Details are kept about how a concern was raised, how it was handled and the outcome. Over half of the respondents stated that they reviewed the policy and 61 per cent did so on an annual basis. Many organizations used a combination of personnel specialists, senior management and a working group to review the policy. Individuals who invoked the procedure might be asked if they were satisfied with the way their concerns were dealt with and if they suffered any reprisals. More generally, an attitude survey might be conducted to discover whether staff think that the organizational culture supports the raising of concerns. Monitoring and review are particularly important in the light of the Public Interest Disclosure Act 1998. Put simply,if an internal procedure is defective it may be easier to demonstrate that an external disclosure was reasonable under Sections 43G and 43H ERA 1996 (see chapter 2).

CONCLUSION

Employees are often the first to realize that there may be something seriously wrong within an organization. However, they may not express their concerns because they feel that 'speaking up' would be disloyal to their colleagues or to their employer. They may also fear harassment or victimization. In these circumstances it may be easier to turn a blind eye rather than report what may just be a suspicion of malpractice. Thus in order to prevent problems being overlooked and to avoid legal pitfalls, personnel practitioners should endeavour to devise policies and procedures which both encourage and enable staff to report their concerns. Such a procedure should aim to:

- define the types of concern that it covers. This definition may well be broader than the matters regarded as 'qualifying disclosures' by Section 43B ERA 1996
- explain its relationship to other procedures. For example,that it does not replace harassment or grievance procedures but is intended to cover circumstances which fall outside their remit. It should also be made clear that the disciplinary procedure may be invoked if there are no reasonable grounds for making an allegation
- indicate how and with whom concerns should be raised and the advice and support that is available (both internally and externally)
- allow staff to be accompanied by a representive of their choice at any meetings or interviews connected with the concerns raised
- outline a target timetable for the employer's response and provide feedback on the outcome of any investigation and any action taken
- indicate how staff can take the matter further if they are dissatisfied with the employer's response
- reassure staff that they will be protected from possible reprisals or victimization

Despite all that has been said above,it could be argued that it is not the precise arrangements established by an organization that are significant. What is essential, however, is that employers demonstrate commitment to ethical behaviour at the highest level,that procedures for handling concerns are agreed with employee representatives and communicated to the workforce and that staff are positively encouraged to use them when appropriate.

Certainly those who have introduced whistleblowing procedures see them as contributing to their image as an ethical and efficient organization. They may also be less likely to fall foul of the law.

NOTES

1. See: Public Concern at Work (PCAW), *Policy Pack*, London, 1998.
2. See generally: Winstanley, Diana and Woodall, Jean, *Ethical Issues in Contemporary Human Resource Management*, London, Macmillan, 1999.
3. It has been suggested that an organization's structure may perform a significant role in deciding whether or not to report wrongdoing. See: King, Granville 'The implications of an organization's structure on whistleblowing', *Journal of Business Ethics*, 1999, pp. 315–26.
4. *Industrial Relations Services Employment Review*, no. 685, August 1999.
5. See: *Second Report of the Committee on Standards in Public Life*, London, HMSO, 1996, vol. 1.
6. Institute of Management Foundation, *Introducing a Whistleblowing Policy*, Checklist 072, 1999.
7. Institute of Personnel and Development, *Whistleblowing*, Information Note 32, London, 2000.
8. For example, see the Local Government Management Board's *Confidential Reporting Code*, London, 1998.
9. In September 1996, a survey of whistleblowing procedures used by local councils in relation to financial malpractice and probity was conducted. A confidential questionnaire was posted to the chief executives (or equivalent) of the 432 English and Welsh local authorities. 171 completed questionnaires were returned, giving a participation rate of 40 per cent. See: Lewis, David, 'Raising concerns about financial malpractice and probity: a survey of whistleblowing procedures in local authorities', Centre for Research in Industrial and Commercial Law, Middlesex University, 1996.
10. In May 1996 a postal survey of whistleblowing procedures in *The Times* Top 500 UK firms was conducted. A confidential questionnaire was sent to Heads of Personnel and 109 organizations agreed to participate. See: Lewis,-David 'Report on whistleblowing procedures in *The Times* Top 500 UK Firms', Centre for Research in Industrial and Commercial Law, Middlesex University, 1996.
11. See: Lewis,David and Ellis,Catherine 'Confidential reporting at work: a survey of employer 'hotlines', Centre for Research in Industrial and Commercial Law, Middlesex University, 1999. In the IRS/PCAW survey, twenty-six respondents provided a telephone 'hotline' to enable employees to raise a concern.
12. Section 10 of the Employment Relations Act 1999 gives workers the right to be accompanied when they attend disciplinary or grievance hearings.

6

Whistleblowing in the Health Service

LUCY VICKERS

INTRODUCTION

Whistleblowing has been a particularly topical issue in the National Health Service over recent years. Several cases in which NHS staff have suffered retaliation for blowing the whistle at work have received a large amount of publicity. In the early 1990s Helen Zeitlin and Graham Pink were dismissed after raising concerns about standards of care within the NHS. Zeitlin had mentioned nursing shortages at a public meeting.[1] Although she was ultimately successful in gaining reinstatement after an appeal to the Secretary of State for Health, she did not return to her job, and her case raised awareness of the difficulties facing staff who speak out about standards at work. Graham Pink was dismissed for gross misconduct after publishing in the *Guardian* a series of letters he had written to hospital managers, his MP, the Chief Executive of the NHS, the Secretary of State for Health and the Prime Minister. In these he raised concerns about staffing levels on the ward in which he worked.[2] He also spoke to the local press about his concerns.[3] Pink's employers ultimately conceded that he had been unfairly dismissed. As with Zeitlin, he did not return to his job and his case led to increased fears on the part of nursing staff about the risks involved in voicing concerns. More recently, Dr Stephen Bolsin left the NHS after finding it impossible to continue work after he had raised concerns about high mortality rates following heart surgery on young babies at the Bristol Royal Infirmary.[4] He was proved correct at the subsequent inquiry into the conduct of the surgeons concerned.[5]

Whistleblowing in the NHS is of particular interest because it operates in a political context. The NHS is an institution of key political significance. The principle of good-quality health care, free at the point of delivery, is very important to the public and governments need to be seen to uphold it. Moreover, the NHS has undergone massive organizational change in the last decade,[6] at times without support from the medical profession.[7] Within such a context, full public debate on standards of care within the Health Service is clearly immensely important but it is also politically sensitive. This political dimension to whistleblowing in the health service has only added to the publicity it has generated.

The importance of free speech and whistleblowing within the NHS has been officially recognized on a number of occasions. The first report of the Nolan Committee on Standards in Public Life made recommendations for the introduction of whistleblowing procedures for employees of various public bodies, including the NHS.[8] The NHS Executive has taken action on the issue, publishing its *Guidance for Staff on Relations with the Public and the Media* in 1993. This was updated in August 1999,[9] to reflect the entry into force of the Public Interest Disclosure Act 1998 (henceforward PIDA 1998). This Act, which provides employment protection for public-interest whistleblowers, reflects the fact that the importance of whistleblowing has now gained wide recognition in the Health Service and beyond.

WHISTLEBLOWING AND PATIENT CONFIDENTIALITY

Any discussion about whistleblowing and NHS staff has to take into account the unique circumstances that operate in the Health Service and, in particular,the strong duty of confidence owed to patients. The professional and ethical duty of patient confidentiality is reinforced by contractual duties of confidence owed by staff by virtue of their employment status.[10] A member of staff contemplating blowing the whistle will need to consider the issue of patient confidentiality. However, this duty of confidentiality is not absolute and can be overridden by a duty on staff to uphold the wider public interest. Whether the public interest requires a disclosure of information or the preservation of confidence is not always obvious and depends on a variety of factors.

PROFESSIONAL DUTY OF CONFIDENCE

The right of patients to confidence in respect of medical matters is well established and is most famously traced to the Hippocratic Oath of the fifth century BC. More recently, it is confirmed by the

United Kingdom Central Council for Nursing, Midwifery and
Health Visiting (UKCC) and the General Medical Council
(GMC), the bodies that govern the professional conduct of the
nursing and medical professions.

There are two main reasons for upholding patient confidence.
First, information relating to health is very often of a personal and
private nature. Confidence should be upheld out of respect for
patient autonomy, privacy and human integrity. Secondly, patient
confidence needs to be upheld for the more practical reason that
patients should not be deterred from seeking medical treatment
for fear that confidence will be breached. Encouraging patients to
come forward for treatment is essential not only for the individual's health but for general public health too. If infectious
diseases or certain mental illnesses are left untreated, this can
represent a risk to public health or safety. A fear that confidence
will be breached could deter patients with such conditions from
seeking the medical attention they both need and deserve. For
both these reasons, it is right that confidentiality in respect of
patient information is strictly observed.

However, the duty of confidence is subject to exceptions when
it is in the public interest to disclose information. The interaction
between the duty to serve the public interest and the duty to
uphold patient confidence is complex. It is dealt with by both the
UKCC Code of practice and the GMC Guidance for doctors.

The UKCC Code of Practice:[11] the UKCC Code of Professional
Conduct sets out the standards expected of nursing staff. Breach
of the Code can lead to loss of registration with the UKCC,
which in turn could lead to loss of employment because NHS
employers require staff to be registered with their respective
governing body. On confidentiality, the Code tells staff to 'protect
all confidential information concerning patients and clients
obtained in the course of professional practice and make disclosures only with consent, where required by the order of a court or
where you can justify disclosure in the wider public interest'
(clause 10). In addition, staff should 'report to an appropriate
person or authority any circumstances in which safe and appropriate care for patients and clients cannot be provided' (clause 12).

Several matters are worth noting in relation to these clauses.
Most obvious is the reference in clause 10 to the public interest.

The importance of protecting patient confidence is clear but the possibility of the public interest overriding that confidence is acknowledged and provided for. Significantly, the clause states that the individual nurse is to be the judge of the public interest. This may be helpful to the whistleblower, as the nurse who breaches confidence in the genuine belief that the public interest is served by the disclosure will not infringe the UKCC Code.

Clause 10 does not provide clear examples for the nurse about when the public interest might be served by disclosure. However, clause 12 of the Code suggests that nurses are not expected to tolerate low standards of care and should raise concerns in this regard. Additionally, the 1996 UKCC Guidelines for Professional Practice make clear that matters such as the standards of care offered by the NHS and concerns about the practical implications of shortages of resources are the legitimate concern of nursing staff and should not be ignored. The suggestion from the UKCC code and guidelines is that raising concerns, or blowing the whistle, about standards of care in the NHS may serve the public interest and may therefore give rise to a legitimate restriction on the duty of patient confidentiality

The GMC Guidance: as with the UKCC Code, the GMC puts primacy on the duty of confidence owed to patients while discussing circumstances in which confidential information can be disclosed, for example where there is patient consent or where disclosure is ordered by a court. The GMC also includes a duty to disclose in the general public interest but this is more narrowly defined than in the UKCC code. It provides that information may be disclosed in the public interest where the failure to disclose could put someone at risk of death or serious harm.[12] There is no suggestion here that raising a matter of concern about general standards of care would be covered under this part of the guidelines. This is not to say that doctors will never be allowed to raise such concerns but they would need to be raised without breaching an individual's confidence, by ensuring that no patient details are divulged.

LEGAL DUTY OF CONFIDENCE

In addition to the professional duty of confidence, legal duties also apply. All employees owe a contractual duty of confidence to the employer, a duty which could be breached if negative comments were made publicly about the workplace.[13] Moreover, an equitable duty of confidence will be owed to patients arising out of the relationship of medical professional and patient. Such a duty arises whenever information is provided to another party in circumstances of confidence.[14] Whether it is based on contract or equity, the legal duty of confidence is always subject to an exception when disclosure serves the public interest.[15] Exactly when the public interest demands disclosure will depend on a number of factors, the most relevant being the nature of the information and the identity of the person to whom disclosure is made.[16]

The more serious the information disclosed, the more likely that any disclosure will be in the public interest. Disclosures of illegal conduct, such as fraud, financial irregularities, corruption or breach of health and safety standards at work are most likely to serve the public interest and so will not breach confidence. In contrast, where concerns do not specifically relate to wrongdoing, the public interest may not be directly served by disclosure. This may cause difficulties for some NHS whistleblowers, as the issues they raise tend to relate to matters such as mismanagement and complaints regarding lack of funding, managerial support or staffing levels.[17] These do not amount to legal wrongs even though they are of a serious nature. It can be argued that the public interest should be interpreted to include such concerns, particularly because of the political importance of such information. However, it is not clear that such reasoning would be accepted by the courts.

The second main factor used to determine whether a particular disclosure is in the public interest or not is the identity of the person or organization to whom the information is given. While it may be in the public interest that the information is revealed to someone, it is not necessarily the case that the public interest is served by general disclosure. In particular, disclosure to the press is difficult to justify. Internal disclosure involves a lesser breach of employer confidence, if any, and so should be easy to justify. In between these two comes disclosure to an external regulatory body, such as the UKCC or the GMC, which itself treats the matter as confidential and so limits wider disclosure. Such action would be justifiable if the concern is of a type that is suitable for investigation by the body to whom the disclosure is made.[19]

The scope of the duty of confidence in relation to medical confidentiality has been considered by the courts on several occasions. In *W v Egdell*,[20] a schizophrenic had been detained for killing five people in a shooting incident. W's case was to be reviewed by a mental health review tribunal, and his solicitors sought a medical report from Dr Egdell for use in those proceedings. The report stated that the patient was still dangerous and raised a number of new concerns that had not been raised by the medical team advising the Home Office about W's future care. As a result, W withdrew his application from the tribunal and the report was not used. Dr Egdell was concerned that the content of the report should be known by W's medical team and by the Home Office, so he sent a copy to both parties without W's consent. W was unsuccessful in his claim that this was a breach of his confidence. The Court of Appeal held that the public interest in the parties knowing the contents of the report overrode any breach of confidence involved. Various factors influenced this decision. First, the identity of the recipient was important. The information was only disclosed to other professionals involved in W's care. The point was made that disclosure for other purposes, for example, in an academic journal, would not have been in the public interest. Secondly, the new information contained in the report was that W maintained a strong interest in home-made bombs and explosives. Information of such seriousness needed to be disclosed for the protection of public safety.

By way of contrast, in *X v Y*[21] the courts upheld the duty of confidence. The case involved two doctors who were continuing to practise despite the fact that they had AIDS. These doctors sought an injunction to prevent publication of their names in an article in a national newspaper. The Court held that the public interest was not served by disclosure of their names. The public interest in encouraging patients to seek treatment for the disease overrode the public interest in debate about the disease and the freedom of the press. Again the two factors identified above were relevant. Because disclosure was to the media, the widest possible form of disclosure,the public interest would need to be very strong indeed for such disclosure to be justified. Moreover, the issue to which the information related was a matter of public interest and required public debate but details of individuals were not needed for that discussion to take place effectively.

WHISTLEBLOWING AND THE DUTY OF CONFIDENCE

Taking into account the factors that influence the scope of the public interest, it becomes evident that some NHS whistleblowers may have difficulty showing that breaching their duty of confidence is justified. For those who raise concerns about specific incidents of inadequate care, incompetence, wrongdoing or illegality, it may be relatively easy to show that the public interest is served, particularly if concerns are raised via internal channels or with a regulatory body such as the UKCC or GMC in the first instance. Greater difficulty is faced by those who wish to use their experience at work to highlight concerns about more general issues such as standards of care, waiting times or the impact of structural change within the NHS. These staff will need to raise concerns in public and the issues are less likely to be categorized as urgent, both factors that militate against a finding that the public interest is served by disclosure.

However, two arguments can be used to support the proposition that disclosures in these circumstances serve the public interest. First, the political dimension to public debate on standards of care in the NHS could be highlighted. Any such debate needs a public forum if it is to be worthwhile and so public disclosure is, arguably, appropriate. Secondly, the extent of any breach of confidence involved should be considered. Disclosure of names, addresses of patients and treatments given would clearly be a major breach of confidence; the public interest would need to be overwhelming for it to be justified. By way of contrast, disclosing that a treatment was carried out, without naming the patient, can more easily be shown to be in the public interest. In such a case the general public will not know who is referred to even though the patient and close relatives may. Discussion of health care standards without reference to particular incidents is likely be very vague and any criticisms hard to substantiate. Allowing a doctor or nurse to refer, even obliquely, to incidents occurring in day to day medical practice may be necessary to add weight to any general discussion on standards of care. Arguably,the general public interest in full public debate on the NHS is served by limited disclosure of this type.

The legal and professional duties of confidence clearly enjoy a significant area of overlap. The only real distinction is that under the professional duty contained in the UKCC code the individual nurse is the judge of the public interest, whereas in law the decision would be made by a court. Clearly, this could cause some difficulty for a nurse whose view taken at the time of disclosure is not subsequently upheld by a court. Any nurse contemplating blowing the whistle in circumstances which might involve a breach of confidence should therefore seek legal advice before doing so to be sure of complying with both legal and professional obligations.

WHISTLEBLOWING AND NHS POLICY

Until the recent publicity about whistleblowing in the Health Service led to change, medical staff had fairly limited encouragement to report concerns about standards of care. The main route was via the regulatory mechanism of the GMC and the UKCC, the bodies through which medical staff are held to account.[22] In addition, individual hospital trusts have grievance and complaints procedures though which concerns can be raised. Set against this is the evidence that increasingly restrictive confidentiality clauses have been issued by the new NHS Trusts exercising their rights under the 1990 legislation to set their own terms and conditions of employment.

The increasing public concern about whistleblowing in the Health Service, in the light of the Zeitlin and Pink cases, eventually led to a response from the NHS Executive. In 1993 it issued its *Guidance for Staff on Relations with the Public and the Media*. This confirms that NHS staff have a right and duty to raise matters of concern, and recognizes that free expression of views can lead to an improvement in the health service. It also requires management to create systems to encourage the reporting of concerns.[23] The procedure recommended by the *Guidance* is that staff should first raise matters informally with their line manager. Only if the informal procedure is ineffective should the matter be raised formally through the management line or through a senior officer designated to hear such matters. The *Guidance* refers to disclosures to the media and states that this will give rise to disciplinary action if unjustified.

Further steps were taken in 1995 when the NHS Executive published its *Code of Practice on Openness in the NHS*.[24] This sets out the obligations on general practitioners and hospitals to provide information to the public on request. The Code allows for extensive disclosure of information but it includes several exceptions, some of which could be construed fairly widely.[25] The information it envisages disclosing is mainly factual information, including information relating to services provided, targets set and achieved, and details of public meetings and complaints procedures. Despite its rather narrow remit, it promotes the idea that openness is beneficial to the health service and it creates a wider set of information that will not be counted as confidential if disclosed.

The change of government in 1997 brought some new initiatives from the government and the NHS Executive. In September 1997, Alan Milburn, then Minister of State for Health, wrote to all Chairs of NHS Trusts and Chairs of Health Authorities emphasizing the importance of free speech for the NHS and requesting that 'gagging clauses' be removed from the employment contracts of staff. Although staff are employed by the Trusts and not by the government, this instruction should lead to the removal of some of the more draconian confidentiality clauses under which some staff operate. In addition, the government supported the passage of the Private Member's Bill which became PIDA 1998.

In August 1999 the NHS Executive published a circular on whistleblowing which was designed to help NHS trusts implement PIDA 1998.[26] This was sent to health authorities together with a resource pack containing model whistleblowing procedures and policies, training and promotional materials and details of a free helpline for NHS staff.[27] This demonstrated a practical commitment to improving the position of whistleblowers in the NHS. The circular requires all health authorities to put into place local policies and procedures by which staff can raise concerns. Any policy must designate a senior manager or non-executive director to deal with matters that have to be raised outside the usual management chain and staff are to be provided with guidance on how to raise concerns about malpractice reasonably and responsibly. The policy must also make clear that concerns will be treated seriously and staff must be protected against victimization for raising the concern. The circular also confirms again that 'gagging clauses' are not to be used.

THE PUBLIC INTEREST DISCLOSURE ACT 1998 AND ITS APPLICATION TO THE NHS

The legal position of those who blow the whistle is discussed in chapter 2. In summary, employees may face discipline or dismissal for what is perceived to be a breach of the duty of trust and confidence contained, expressly or by implication, in the employment contract. The introduction of PIDA 1998 has improved the position of such employees enormously, providing a remedy where disclosure is made in accordance with its terms. Protection against dismissal or other adverse treatment is provided to workers as long as the subject matter of the disclosure is covered by the legislation and a suitable procedure is used (see chapter 2). PIDA 1998 covers all employees, regardless of length of service. It also covers other workers who are not employees, including agency workers, and doctors, dentists, ophthalmologists and pharmacists working for the NHS.

THE SUBJECT MATTER OF DISCLOSURE

Disclosures relating to issues of concern to the NHS are likely to come within the protection afforded by PIDA 1998 as the matters protected include a danger to health and safety. Because this does not require imminent danger, general concerns about levels of funding or mismanagement can be covered as well as more immediate matters, such as disclosures about the competence of particular members of staff. A second category of information that may be relevant to NHS whistleblowing is where people have failed, are failing or are likely to fail to comply with a legal obligation to which they are subject. NHS Trusts owe countless legal obligations, not only to provide health care but also, as employers, not to discriminate on grounds of sex, race or disability and not to dismiss unfairly.[28] Additionally, as public authorities they must make decisions reasonably and comply with both natural justice and the Human Rights Act 1998. Exactly how courts will interpret the list of 'qualifying disclosures' contained in PIDA 1998 is yet to be seen. However, the breadth of the provisions means that most issues that are raised by NHS staff, whether they are disclosures of wrongdoing or more general policy concerns, are likely to be covered.

THE PROCESS OF DISCLOSURE

Internal disclosure: disclosure within the organization will be automatically protected. All that is required on the part of employees is that they act in good faith, in that they honestly suspect that the malpractice has occurred. In addition, for NHS staff, raising concerns with the employing Trust and even directly with the Department of Health is treated in the same way as internal disclosure. This is significant, because staff can feel reluctant to raise concerns with their immediate manager, particularly where concerns involve explicit or implicit criticism of individual staff or management in general. It is to be hoped that after the introduction of PIDA 1998, NHS staff will feel safer raising concerns internally. If concerns are not adequately dealt with, or if the staff member fears retaliation, this may give grounds for a protected external disclosure.

Under PIDA 1998 disclosures made to certain prescribed bodies are treated as internal disclosures, with the additional requirement that the worker must believe the allegation to be true.[29] The Secretary of State has prescribed a number of regulatory bodies for the purposes of PIDA 1998 but they do not include the GMC or UKCC, or any body specifically for health service concerns. However, the Audit Commission is prescribed to receive concerns about fraud or value for money in the health service and matters which may affect health and safety at work can be reported to the Health and Safety Executive. The lack of a specific body prescribed for health service concerns is therefore not as large a lacuna in the protection offered by PIDA 1998 as at first appears, particularly as disclosures made directly to the Department of Health are treated as internal disclosures.

External disclosure: if a concern is raised internally but no action or inadequate action is taken, the employee may be justified in raising the concern externally. However,greater conditions are attached – the employee needs to have a reasonable belief in the truth of the allegation, act in good faith and not act for personal gain. As a general rule, a concern must first be raised internally or with a specified regulator. The only exceptions to this are where employees reasonably believe that they will be victimized if they make the disclosure internally, or reasonably believe that evidence will be destroyed or concealed if raised internally, and there is no regulatory body with whom to raise the concern.

The final condition on external disclosure is that the disclosure must be reasonable, and PIDA 1998 sets out factors that will be considered in assessing reasonableness. The factors echo those used to determine where the public interest lies and include the identity of the person to whom disclosure is made and the seriousness of the issue. For external disclosure to be reasonable, the issue will need to be very serious. A further factor relevant in the context of the NHS is whether disclosure is made in breach of a duty of confidence owed by the employer to any other person. Disclosures that breach patient confidentiality will be less likely to be reasonable, but this is not to say that that they will never be reasonable. In circumstances where a court will find the public interest served by disclosure, an employment tribunal is likely to find external disclosure reasonable.

CONCLUSION

Full protection for whistleblowers is, to an extent, dependent on a change in the culture of the workplace. Whistleblowers need to be viewed as conscientious employees with something important to say, rather than as troublemakers who upset the good order of the workplace. Without a change in workplace culture,which is a slow process, the practical impact of the measures outlined above may well be limited. However, PIDA 1998, the new NHS Executive guidance on whistleblowing in the NHS and the professional codes of conduct together should improve the position of whistleblowers in the health service, even if they cannot solve all the difficulties they face. The codes of practice make clear that staff have a professional duty to raise matters of concern. Staff should feel safer to raise concerns in the knowledge that their employment status will be protected if they do so. The introduction of new guidance on the importance of free speech in the NHS may even be able to start the process of change towards a culture where the contribution of staff to open discussion and debate is truly valued.

NOTES

1. Independent, 10 September 1993.
2. *Guardian*, 11 April 1990
3. *Stockport Express Advertiser*, 25 July 1990. See also: Pink, Graham, *Whistleblowing: for whom the truth hurts*, London, *Guardian* and Charter 88, 1992.
4. *Guardian*, 30 May 1998.
5. Confirmed by the Secretary of State for Health H.C. Deb., 18 June 1998 Cols. 529–30.
6. The National Health Service and Community Care Act 1990 created new NHS hospital trusts. It introduced an internal market to the NHS. The internal market is now being dismantled after the change of government in 1997.
7. The BMA campaigned against the 1990 changes.
8. *First Report of the Committee on Standards in Public Life*, London, HMSO, 1995.
9. *The Public Interest Disclosure Act 1998: Whistleblowing in the NHS*, NHS Executive, HSC 1999/198, 27 August 1999.
10. Also, some medical staff owe special duties of confidence imposed by statute or legal regulation. For example, The Human Fertilisation and Embryology Act 1990 Section 33 and The National Health Service (Venereal Diseases) Regulations 1974, Regulation 2.
11. The third edition of the UKCC Code of Professional Conduct was published in 1992.
12. Paragraph 18, *Guidance for Doctors: Confidentiality*, London, GMC, 1995.
13. *Faccenda Chicken v Fowler [1986] ICR 297.*
14. *Coco v A.N. Clark (Engineers) Ltd [1969] RPC 41.*
15. *Initial Services v Putterill [1968] QB 398.*
16. For detail on factors that can affect the interpretation of the public interest see: Cripps, Yvonne, *The Legal Implications of Disclosure in the Public Interest*, London, Sweet & Maxwell, 1994.
17. These were the most common concerns expressed by nursing staff contacting the RCN Whistleblow Scheme. See: *Whistleblow: Report on the Work of the RCN Whistleblow Scheme*, London, RCN, 1992.
18. *Attorney-General v Guardian Newspapers No. 2[1988] 3 WLR 776.*
19. *Re a company's application [1989] 2 All ER 248.* See also: *Woolgar v (1) Chief Constable of Sussex Police (2) UKCC [1999] 3 AER 604* where the public interest was served by disclosure of confidential information by the police to the UKCC.
20. *[1990] 2 WLR 471.*
21. *[1988] 2 All ER 648 QBD.*
22. Hunt,Geoff *Whistleblowing in the Health Service: Accountability, Law and Professional Practice*, London, Edward Arnold, 1995, chapters 3 and 4.
23. Paragraphs 3 and 5.
24. NHS Executive, April 1995.
25. Exceptions include confidential patient information, information relating to internal discussion and advice, and management information. These categories are not defined and, if broadly interpreted, could extend widely.

26. *The Public Interest Disclosure Act 1998: Whistleblowing in the NHS*, HSC 1999/198, London, 27 August 1999.

27. This resource pack was produced by Public Concern at Work.

28. Sex Discrimination Act 1975, Race Relations Act 1976, Disability Discrimination Act 1995, Employment Rights Act 1996.

29. Public Interest Disclosure (Prescribed Persons) Order 1999 (SI 1999 No. 1549).

7
Whistleblowing and Local Government
STEPHEN HOMEWOOD

This chapter outlines the role and methods of encouraging whistleblowing in local government in England and Wales. Current policy and the impact of recent legislative changes will be considered. The chapter concludes with an assessment of the possible impact of the Human Rights Act 1998 (HRA 1998) and the proposed Freedom of Information Bill, together with some comments and proposals for change.

INTRODUCTION

Local government is a large and heterogeneous part of public administration. It has undergone a great deal of change in recent years and is likely, following proposed new legislation, to see further significant changes. It is not possible to understand the current and proposed system, and thus the role and importance of whistleblowing in local government, without an understanding of the broader constitutional developments taking place in the United Kingdom. Equally, we will need to consider other legislative and policy issues, not necessarily directed at local government, in order to assess the role and impact of whistleblowing in this area.

It should be acknowledged at the outset that there is a fundamental tension between central control by the state and the need for some form of local government. The drive for an efficient and fair administration is closely linked to the development of accountability within local authorities. It is also important to remember that they are elected bodies and to consider how this factor affects the key themes of accountability and efficiency in local government.

THE STRUCTURE OF LOCAL GOVERNMENT

Some form of local government has always existed in the U K but the extent to which it is merely there to carry out local administration is open to question. From the early developments in Norman times until quite recently local government essentially consisted of the Justices of the Peace, who carried out a variety of administrative functions as well as that of deciding questions of law.[1] It was only with the Municipal Corporations Act 1835 and the extensions to the voting franchise that we see the beginning of the modern system.

Local government changed little from the major reforms of the 1880s until the Local Government Act 1972 (LGA 1972). London local government, which was always an exception, had been reformed in the 1960s. The Greater London Council (GLC), which took a more strategic view of matters (such as transport) and left the 32 London Boroughs to take on the day to day work, became a useful model for other large conurbations. The LGA 1972 introduced Metropolitan County Councils (MCCs) with their smaller metropolitan districts. The rest of England was divided up into non-metropolitan counties and districts. Similarly, Wales had its counties and districts.

The Local Government Act 1985 signalled a major change in the work and structure of local authorities. The abolition of the GLC and the MCCs was a major constitutional event – no previous elected bodies had been removed without being replaced. In their place came a number of government appointed or nominated bodies to carry out some of their functions, with the remainder being pushed 'downwards' to the districts and boroughs. After further modifications in the early 1990s the current situation in England is as follows: 34 county councils, 33 London boroughs, 36 metropolitan districts, 238 district councils and 46 unitary councils. In Wales there are 22 unitary districts.

It is worth noting the recent development of devolution for Scotland, Wales and Northern Ireland, with their new Parliament and Assemblies. Although the powers they have been given are complex and differ as between each devolved body, it is clear that they will have a major effect on the work and responsibilities of local authorities. Equally, the introduction of the Regional Development Agencies and their possible Assemblies, will have an important impact on the work of existing local authorities and constitute, in effect, another layer of local government. Finally, we have the new Greater London Authority taking over a strategic role. Our observations about whistleblowing procedures are also relevant to these new bodies.

THE FUNCTIONS OF LOCAL AUTHORITIES

All the powers and duties of local authorities derive from legislation, whether it be local government statutes or from legislation dealing with the various parts of the modern state, such as housing, education, planning or environmental controls. In theory, we elect councillors to decide local policy and to administer many of these services and it is arguable that the impact of the work of local government on our daily lives is far more direct than that of the central state.

However, since the 1980s many of the functions of local authorities have slowly, but inexorably, been removed. Under the Local Government Act 1985, authorities were required to put out for tender the performance of a range of functions and many were 'contracted out' under the compulsory competitive tendering (CCT) system. This led to the the service being performed by other organizations, including private companies. These changes ensured that there was a move from delivery by the local authority to the role of 'facilitator'; awarding contracts for services and then monitoring performance under them. In addition, a number of former services, such as the provision of housing and further and higher education, were simply removed to other providers. This process has raised questions as to the democratic and financial accountability of local government. Arguably, we have moved in many areas from the traditional model of scrutiny by the public via annual elections to a system of checking and enforcement of contractual relations, with some loss of accountability for the services provided.

Further development of central control resulted from the increased financial and audit controls imposed on local government. The provision of powers to 'cap' local revenue raising powers under the Rates Act 1984, the fixed controls on expenditure and the ever-increasing amount of quasi-legislation in the form of government circulars and 'guidance' has meant that, in reality, local government has been left with little discretion. It is claimed that local authorities have become much more of a local administration than a local government. This raises questions about the extent to which local wishes and proposals can be adequately represented and delivered by elected councillors. Recent proposals to 'modernize' local government are a reflection of concerns about local democracy but in themselves may not adequately deal with the inherent tension between central controls and local wishes.

ACCOUNTABILITY AND SCRUTINY

Regular elections are clearly one method of ensuring some form of political accountability. The replacement of representatives allows for the most direct response by the electorate. However, the extent to which elections actually control the local authority is often more theoretical than real. The very low turnout for local elections and the control often imposed by the political party system leaves this form of democracy open to doubt. Many areas of the country have local authorities which have remained in the hands of one party or group for generations. The possibilities for corrupt or unlawful activities are plain when there is so little effective scrutiny. Thus the government has proposed some changes to try to remedy this situation (see below).

Earlier attempts to control the misuse of power and possible corruption in public office are to be found in the Prevention of Corruption Acts of 1906 and 1916. Under these statutes, it is an offence for employees to corruptly receive any gifts or inducements to do anything or refrain from doing things in their official capacity or show favours. If employees receive anything from those seeking or holding contracts, the courts will treat this as corruption unless the individual can prove the contrary. The Local Government Act 1972 requires that if any officer has a pecuniary interest in a contract she or he must declare it. However, problems have occurred in deciding what a pecuniary interest is and, if a declaration is made, what role an officer can then play in the decision-making process.

While the courts have long been able to control illegal activity, from about the early 1970s they became increasingly willing to oversee the legality of decision-making in all public bodies. In theory, judicial review procedures provide a mechanism to scrutinize the legal powers being exercised by local authorities. However, in practice, this remedy is costly, often difficult to obtain and thus rarely sought. Even if one succeeds, the remedies available are often inappropriate and an authority may avoid liability if an application for review is not brought almost immediately.

These sorts of problem were part of the inspiration to look to Scandinavia for a quicker and cheaper method to check the work of local authorities. This resulted in the introduction of Commissioners for Local Administration (ombudspersons) under the Local Government Act 1974. Their role is to investigate whether there has been any injustice caused by maladministration and to make public reports on their findings. Although generally successful, the ombudspersons are excluded from a number of areas of local government and cannot legally enforce their decisions. They provide an effective threat because local authorities are required to publish ombudspersons' reports and their responses to them.

The financial check on income and expenditure carried out by the Audit Commission is a key feature of accountability and much valuable work is carried out by the regular internal audit in exposing irregularities and fraud. The annual reports and advice given by the Audit Commission have proved essential in curbing some of the ways in which local authorities have carried out their work.

All methods of monitoring the work of public authorities require an adequate flow of information and much can be gleaned from the reports of both the ombudsmen and the Audit Commission. The push to make the work of local authorities more transparent was given a major boost by the Local Government Act 1972. Section 100 of this Act deals with the admission of the public and the press (with some exceptions) to committee meetings. In addition, the Local Government (Access to Information) Act 1985 extends the public's right to see the papers and documentation used to inform the decisions of many committees. There are also specific provisions to ensure greater openness, for example, in relation to the environment and planning. Thus the fact that most licensing and planning decisions must be entered in registers provides a great deal of transparency. Unfortunately, difficulties occur in relation to the accuracy of such registers, their complexity and charges, and the fact that very few people are aware of their existence.

Finally, it is worth noting the position of the Monitoring Officer, introduced by the Local Government and Housing Act

1989. The role of this officer was to act as an internal watchdog and to deal with complaints relating to any proposal or decision, made by any committee or office holder, which might give rise to any contravention of the law or code of practice, or any malad-ministration.[2] Monitoring Officers are required to report such concerns to the Chief Financial Officer or Head of Paid Service (with a copy to all the council) and the authority must suspend action on these matters until they are resolved. However, evidence to the Nolan Committee suggested that Monitoring Officers have not been used much.[3] Few reports appear to have been made and therefore questions arise as to their effectiveness.

CODES OF CONDUCT

One strategy to improve probity has been the introduction of Codes of Practice for local government officers and elected coun-cillors. In relation to the latter, earlier concerns about possible misuse of powers had led to the recommendation that Rules of Conduct be developed. Following earlier proposals, the Widdi-combe Committee on 'The Conduct of Local Authority Business' recommended that the code should be given statutory status and that new councillors should be made to declare that they would abide by it on taking up their posts. The Local Government and Housing Act 1989, Sections 30 and 31 require such a National Code of Local Government Conduct to be drawn up and also require all councillors to abide by it. Breach of the code may constitute maladministration and, if such a finding is made, the ombudsperson will identify the councillor and give information on the breach. The information made available here could be of potential significance as it might lead to further action being taken by the local authority or by those who have suffered maladminis-tration. However, as Craig points out, we should not just focus on the ombudsmen, 'but also upon internal grievance procedures which are used by several authorities' to gauge the availability of obtaining redress for the complainant and ensuring standards are maintained.[4]

In relation to officers or employees, local authorities were not required to draw up codes of conduct but could do so on a volun-tary basis. In fact, as recent research by the Local Government Association (henceforward LGA) has shown, at present some 87 per cent of local authorities have drawn up such codes for their employees.[5] These codes are usually incorporated into contracts of employment and failure to abide by the code could result in disciplinary procedures being used. The failure might also be used as evidence in criminal proceedings if abuse of position has taken place.[6] The LGA survey also found that about two-thirds of local authorities had introduced a whistleblowing policy (or were in the process of so doing so) which was based on the draft code issued by the Local Government Management Board (see below).

REPORT OF THE NOLAN COMMITTEE

In spite of the range of controls on local authorities, much dissatisfaction remained about the way in which they performed their work. Although there seem to have been very few clear cases of corruption, inquiries into certain councils (such as Brent and North Cornwall) revealed that some matters were dealt with badly and that there was a wide divergence of practice between councils. Concerns seem to have focused particularly on the area of planning and the huge amounts of money involved in gaining consent for development. Attention also focused on the single-party control of some councils.

In 1997 the Nolan Committee on Standards in Public Life turned its attention to examine local government (Nolan 1997). As well as re-emphasizing the seven principles of good practice and finding that local authorities generally maintained high standards of conduct, the Committee recommended a number of changes, many of which are now being adopted. One important recommendation was that whistleblowing procedures should be introduced. Another was that there should be local codes of good practice drawn up to supplement the 1994 National Code of Conduct for Local Government Employees.[7]

Also in 1997, the former Local Government Management Board produced a *Confidential Reporting Code*. This provides a model which takes into account most of the requirements of the Public Interest Disclosure Act 1998 (henceforward PIDA 1998) and can be adopted as a whole or modified for local circumstances. The Confidential Reporting Code applies to all employees and contractors and suppliers of services to councils. It also aims to ensure 'the highest standards of openness, probity and accountability' and is intended to 'encourage and enable employees to raise serious concerns within the council rather than overlooking a problem or blowing the whistle outside'.[8] It is clearly stated that the code does not replace existing corporate complaints procedures which may well provide a valuable method for dealing with allegations of harmful or illegal activities within the authority.

Under the code, concerns may be raised anonymously and will be treated in confidence. Depending on its seriousness, a concern may be addressed to the Chief Executive of the Council, the Chief Financial Officer, the Monitoring Officer or to an internal auditor. The code also makes it clear that there will be no harassment or victimization and steps will be taken to protect the complainant when allegationss are made in good faith but prove to be unfounded.[9] However, if a complaint is made frivolously, maliciously or for personal gain, disciplinary action will be taken. Finally, although employees are not expected to prove beyond doubt any of the issues of concern, reasonable grounds will have to be demonstrated. If the complainant is not satisfied with the council's response and the person 'feels it is right to take the matter outside the Council', the code offers advice as to who might be consulted, including a designated person identified by the Council, the district auditor, a trade union or the police.[10]

The code appears to reflect many of the principles upon which PIDA 1998 is based (see chapter 2). It is written in a relatively clear and accessible style and provides practical guidance. However, it says little about enforcement, how it might overlap with certain statutory duties, for example to report to auditors, or what is meant by good faith or reasonableness. Although it applies to all local government employees, it says little about councillors, who may also suffer reprisals if they 'blow the whistle'. The fact that it is voluntary also raises certain doubts.

RECENT DEVELOPMENTS

Dissatisfaction with the direction that local government had been taking led the Labour government to carry out a fundamental review of the structure, constitution and organization of local authorities. When enacted,the Local Government Bill 2000 will introduce major changes to the ways in which local councils will be governed, elected and paid. It is claimed that, in order to make authorities more effective, efficient and economical, they should move to a more executive or cabinet style of local government, with mayors possibly being directly elected after a referendum. The remainder of elected councillors would act as a scrutiny panel. Criticisms have been made of this proposal. In particular that, while the new system might be more efficient, it may not fit well with proposals for more transparency and openness.[11] Decisions will be made by a small cabinet, leaving doubt as to the extent of consultation and criticism which may be made of proposals until after they are agreed. Equally, how effective will the scrutiny be if the majority of other councillors are from the same political party?

For our purposes, the new ethical framework proposed in Part II of the Local Government Bill 2000 is particularly important. Following a recommendation in the Nolan Report, it is proposed that standards committees should be set up in each local authority to deal with complaints against councillors. In addition, a new statutory local code of conduct for councillors should be produced to replace the 1994 version. This should be based on a model code with principles of good conduct in it to be specified by Ministers or the National Assembly for Wales. Parts of the code will be mandatory and others left to local adaptation. Further, it is proposed that there will be a separate and independent National Standards Board for England and Wales which will investigate all written allegations of breaches of the local codes. Ethical Standards Officers will investigate the complaint and a separate Adjudication Panel will be established with power to enforce a range of penalties, including suspension or disqualification from office for a maximum of 5 years. Additionally, after consultation a new code of conduct for employees will be drawn up to reflect the changes in the work of local government. This will then be incorporated into the terms and conditions of employment of local government staff. By introducing a statutory form of whistleblowing good practice as well as the codes, these proposals clearly go beyond what is required by PIDA 1998.

Having considered the latest proposals relating to standards in local government, it is worth briefly considering some of the other changes in the structure and organization of local government which are envisaged because they reflect a change of emphasis and an attempt to improve local democracy. The CCT system is being replaced from January 2000 by a system known as 'Best Value'. Many 'had lost confidence in the ability of the CCT to deliver the promised better value services' (Cirell and Bennett,1999). According to these commentators, the concept of 'Best Value' is to be regarded as more than simply a replacement for CCT and should be seen as a part of the major constitutional reform promised by the Labour government. The Local Government Act 1999 (henceforward LGA 1999) not only changes the CCT system but envisages local authorities as bodies 'leading their communities' by taking the key role in initiating and coordinating policies rather than necessarily delivering the services themselves. Although this sounds familiar, the LGA 1999 places emphasis on cooperation and partnerships with other public and private bodies, including the new Regional Development Agencies and the not for profit sector.

The other major reform envisaged by the government was that of the 'governance' function of local authorities. The Local Government Bill 2000 emphasizes new structures, possibly following the model of the Greater London Act of 1999, with its elected mayor and small executive who are to be scrutinized by the Greater London Assembly. Other constitutional changes involve the number and form of local elections and attempt to encourage greater participation by the electorate. It is claimed that if it is made easier to vote, elections are more frequent and are perhaps organized on a proportional system, turnout will increase and there will be more effective scrutiny of those elected. The government so far seems unenthusiastic about proportional representation, but it has suggested modernizing practices by allowing voting at supermarkets and more postal balloting. Arguably, there are many other reasons why voter turnout is so low, including recognition of the fact that local authorities have lost real discretionary power. Thus these proposals may not lead to a greater turnout of voters.

Because the representative nature of those elected has been doubted, there are also moves to make standing for election as a councillor more attractive. Increased allowances and an enhanced role, particularly for those who become members of the new 'cabinet' or executive committees, may make the job more interesting. Nevertheless, the majority will act as 'backbenchers' and the time needed for a full-time career outside local authority work may continue to deter many from standing. The abilities of councillors have also been questioned and attempts to improve them are being initiated. In the author's opinion, greater improvements in efficiency could be made by more and better training.

Finally, the possible impact of the Human Rights Act 1998 and the Freedom of Information Bill should be considered. In relation to the former, the HRA 1998 will incorporate the European Convention on Human Rights and its jurisprudence into the law of the United Kingdom. All public authorities must ensure that their activities comply with the principles of the Convention as far as it is possible to do so. Article 10 of the Convention, which deals with rights of free speech and expression, is especially relevant to those who work for public bodies. Case law under the Convention has tended to reflect a concern for those whose activities may contribute to the development of democracy and whose freedom of expression must therefore be given special protection. It is clear that this may be of assistance to the potential whistleblower in local government.

The proposals in the Freedom Of Information Bill 2000 may also have an impact on the ethical conduct of public bodies. Citizens already have rights to access certain information held by local authorities,for example under the Local Government (Access to Information) Act 1985, the Data Protection Act 1998 and the Access to Personal Files Act 1987. The focus of the 1999 Bill is on a statutory right of access to information kept by a wide range of organizations, including local government. It will probably include a number of quasi-public bodies and contractors. There will be an independent Information Commissioner to assist with enforcement and appeals available to a tribunal. Clearly, it is assumed that the more information available to the general public, the more transparent will be the activities of the local authority. Hopefully, even with the number of exemptions proposed in the Freedom of Information Bill, there will be more information available and, as a result, fewer possibilities of concealing unethical conduct.

WHISTLEBLOWING TO LOCAL GOVERNMENT

The role of local government includes not just the provision of services but also the regulation and control of a number of activities, such as environmental protection and planning. In order to carry out these activities effectively local government needs a large team of inspectors as well as other officers. Because there are never enough staff or finances to carry out all these functions, avoidance inevitably occurs. It remains an interesting question as to how far the new legislation on whistleblowing will assist local authorities in the detection and prosecution of those who breach the law. Will the new rules enable employees of companies or other bodies, either under some form of contract with the local authority or otherwise, to assist in the detection of unlawful conduct?

CONCLUSION

Local authorities, their councillors and staff are all faced with an overwhelming amount of checks and controls. Given the presence of elections, judicial control, central government scrutiny, codes of conduct, monitoring officers, the Audit Commission, ombudsmen, the right of access to information and the criminal sanctions for corruption, some may suggest that there are sufficient deterrents to wrongdoing. When one adds the new Ethical Standards Committees and Boards, the freedom of information proposals and the impact on local government of the PIDA 1998, it might be asked whether there are more than enough controls on local authorities. However, if one considers the doubts surrounding the interpretation of PIDA 1998 (see chapter 2) and the width of exemptions under the proposed Freedom of Information Act, one might be reluctant to oppose additional measures. Even when new constitutional structures are in place, some would insist that extra protection for whistleblowers is still needed in local government.

On the other hand, if the current moves produce greater electoral scrutiny, a more involved electorate and a critical and effective opposition, it could be argued that these general controls will have as much impact as specific safeguards. Additionally, better paid and more professional councillors with more efficient methods of working might also make a significant contribution to standards of conduct in local government. Indeed, greater emphasis on transparency, the new 'standards' machinery and the possibilities of greater judicial scrutiny using the Human Rights Act 1998, might mean that more may be achieved by these changes than by PIDA 1998.

BIBLIOGRAPHY

Campaign for Freedom of Information, *Greater secrecy results from Local Government Bill*, London, 1998.

Craig, P, *Administrative Law* ,London, Sweet & Maxwell, 1999.

Cirell and Bennett, 'Best value?', *Solicitors Journal*, 1999, pp. 1004–5.

Department of the Environment, *The National Code of Local Government Conduct*, Circular 8/90, London, 1990.

Department of the Environment,Transport and the Regions, *Modernising Local government: In Touch with the People*, CM 4014, London, HMSO, 1998.

Department of the Environment,Transport and the Regions, *Local Leadership, Local Choice*, CM 4298, London, HMSO, 1999.

Local Government Association, *Probity in Planning, Guidance Note*, London, 1997.

Local Government Association, *Modern Local Government, Taking the Initiative, An LGA Survey*,London, 1999.

Local Government Management Board, *The Code of Conduct for Local Government Employees*, London, 1994.

Local Government Management Board, *Confidential Reporting Code for Employees*, London, 1998.

London Borough of Barnet, *Code of Conduct for Employees of Barnet Council*, London, 1995.

Nolan, Lord, *Third Report of the Committee on Standards in Public Life: Standards of Conduct in Local Government in England Scotland and Wales*, Transcripts of Oral Evidence, vol. 2, CM 3702-II, London, HMSO, 1997.

Widdicombe Committee, *The Report of the Committee of Inquiry into the Conduct of Local Authority Business*, CM 9797, London, HMSO, 1986

NOTES

1. They still have this function, for example,in relation to the award of licences.
2. See: Local Government and Housing Act 1989, Section 5.
3. See the Third Report of the Committee on Standards in Public Life, *Standards of Conduct in Local Government in England, Scotland and Wales*, London, HMSO, 1997, CM 3702, vol. 2, p. 25.
4. Craig, P., *Administrative Law* , London, Sweet & Maxwell, 1999, p. 246.
5. Local Government Association, *Modern Local Government, Taking the Initiative, An LGA Survey*, London, 1999, p. 8.
6. See, for example: London Borough of Barnet, *Code of Conduct for Employees of Barnet Council*, London, 1995.
7. This was given statutory force by the Local Government and Housing Act 1989.
8. Local Government Management Board, *Confidential Reporting Code for Employees*, London, 1998, paragraph 1.3.
9. Local Government Management Board, *Confidential Reporting Code for Employees*, London, 1998, paragraph 6.1.

10. Local Government Management Board, *Confidential Reporting Code for Employees*, London, 1998, paragraph 9.1.
11. See: Campaign for Freedom of Information, *Greater secrecy results from Local Government Bill*, London, 1998.

8
Whistleblowing in Education
ANNE RUFF AND DAVID LEWIS

This chapter considers whistleblowing in schools and further and higher education. All educational establishments will be anxious to ensure that impropriety is checked. However, in schools the issue of whistleblowing is linked primarily to child protection and financial management, whereas in further and higher education the issue of academic freedom of speech predominates. The procedures devised in each sector will reflect the importance attached to these matters as well as the different legal and organizational structures of the institutions involved.

SCHOOLS

School teachers are in a position of trust and responsibility in relation to children and young people. A teacher may obtain information about, for example, a parent, a fellow member of staff, a social worker or a priest, which the teacher considers should be disclosed to his or her employer or to another third party. In addition, the increased financial and management responsibilities resting on the head teacher and the governing body as a consequence of devolved spending powers have added to the expectations and demands placed on them. It is essential that whistleblowing procedures allow concerns about the conduct of teachers, members of the governing body, local education authority (henceforward LEA) employees, parents and carers to be freely expressed. However, they must also ensure that individuals who are the subject of allegations are entitled to speedy and fair investigations.

WITH WHOM MIGHT A CONCERN BE RAISED?

The teacher's employer
Who employs a teacher will vary according to the type of school involved and whether or not they work for an agency. Maintained

schools have a governing body which has overall responsibility for the conduct of the school and the LEAs have general responsibility for educational provision in their areas. In the state sector there are three main categories of school: community, voluntary and foundation. For community, voluntary controlled and community special schools the LEA is the employer. The governing body recommends the appointment of a suitable candidate but the LEA may refuse to appoint that person in certain circumstances. The Professional Association of Teachers (henceforward PAT) considers that one reason why teachers have not in the past raised concerns is that the LEA rather than the head teacher is their employer.

In the case of foundation and voluntary aided schools the appointment is made by the governing body as employer but the LEA has an advisory role. However, where the delegated budget has been suspended, for example because it is a failing school, the LEA's consent is required to appoint or dismiss staff. By definition, agency teachers are not employed by either the LEA or the governing body. However, they are protected by the Public Interest Disclosure Act 1998 (henceforward PIDA 1998) because they come within the definition of a 'worker' (see chapter 2). The NUT considers that whistleblowing procedures should apply to all teaching and non-teaching staff, irrespective of their employment status. Finally, it should be noted that city technology colleges and other independent schools may be operated by an individual, a company or a trust, which will be the teacher's employer.

Teachers will be regarded as having made a disclosure to their employer if they follow the procedure authorized by the employer.[1] Where the LEA is the employer, it is likely that the 'Confidential Reporting Code' prepared by the Local Government Management Board (henceforward LGMB) will be followed. This code may also be applied by governing bodies where they are the employer. The code recommends a confidential reporting policy which should, for example:

- be in writing
- provide for matters to be dealt with quickly
- have the support of any recognized trade unions
- state who will deal with the allegations and how they will be dealt with

- do as much as possible to ensure confidentiality for the person raising the concern
- be independent of line management, if necessary
- remind employees that matters can exceptionally be raised externally[2]

The LGMB and the teaching unions consider that the whistle-blowing procedure should be used where an employee has concerns about possible malpractice and it is not appropriate to use other mechanisms, for example, grievance or disciplinary procedures. The LGMB believes that employees should raise concerns either with their line manager or with a designated senior manager, or where neither of these are appropriate with an independent person or organization designated by the local authority.

The National Union of Teachers (NUT), the National Association of Schoolmasters and Union of Women Teachers (NUSUWT) and the Professional Association of Teachers (PAT) have produced guidelines for their members. All three unions emphasize the importance of having agreed internal procedures. Unlike the LGMB which favours internal procedures, albeit independent of line management if necessary, the NUT considers that a whistleblowing procedure should enable complaints to be raised externally to the school. The NASUWT considers that external channels would only be appropriate in exceptional cases. The NUT is also concerned that the procedure should ensure that the person investigating the complaint should, 'while maintaining the confidentiality of the complainant, ensure that any individual who is the subject of the allegation [be] given the details of the allegation in order to respond'.[3] The NASUWT emphasizes the importance of members facing allegations under this procedure being represented and fairly investigated. It also recommends that a whistleblowing procedure should set out clear time limits and that it should be monitored as well as being reviewed annually.[4]

Another responsible person
In accordance with the Employment Rights Act 1996 Section 43C, a teacher may also disclose information to 'another responsible person'. This should facilitate the raising of concerns with the chair of the school's governing body. It is debatable whether it would include disclosure to other individual members of the

governing body unless that individual had specific responsibility for the matters involved. However, reporting a concern to the whole governing body may be permissible because the governing body is a corporate entity having legal personality (and may therefore be said to be a 'person'). The governing body's functions and responsibilities relate to, for example, the conduct of the school, establishing complaints procedures, the use of the school premises and managing the school's budget. Raising concerns with the Director of Education or a local councillor may also be appropriate, because the LEA has overall responsibility for maintained schools in its area. Similarly, a disclosure might be protected if it is made to the chair of the Diocesan Board or similar body in the case of schools with a religious character.

Other potential recipients
PIDA 1998 also permits disclosures to a Minister of the Crown; in the course of obtaining legal advice; to a person prescribed by the Secretary of State; and to any other person in limited circumstances (see chapter 2). These provisions are likely to cover disclosures to the Minister for Schools and the Secretary of State for Education and Employment, as well as concerns raised with a registered inspector leading an Ofsted inspection of the school where the teacher is employed. Disclosures to external bodies, for example the police or the press, are subject to stringent requirements depending on whether or not there has been exceptionally serious wrongdoing. Although this is not defined in the legislation, child abuse would be an obvious example.

WHAT CAN BE DISCLOSED?

A 'qualifying disclosure' is one which a worker reasonably believes tends to show a matter falling into one or more of the following categories:

1 a criminal offence
2 failure to comply with any legal obligation
3 a miscarriage of justice
4 danger to the health and safety of any individual
5 damage to the environment, or
6 the deliberate concealment of information tending to show any of the matters listed above[5]

Teachers are most likely to be concerned about information coming within categories 1, 2, 4 and 6. Since the reporting of health and safety issues should be dealt with in a specialist procedure, we concentrate here on criminal offences and failure to comply with a legal obligation. It should be noted that the NUT believes that PIDA 1998 is too narrow in scope and that whistleblowing procedures should also apply to disclosures relating to other matters, including suspected financial malpractice and breaches of agreed LEA or governing body procedures.

CRIMINAL OFFENCES

Sexual abuse and offences
Disclosure of a criminal offence is likely to be protected only where it relates to the safety of pupils or members of staff, or the management of the school. Sexual or physical abuse of pupils is the most common concern. However, with the increase in devolved budgets, financial crimes may occur. Another area of interest relates to parents falsifying information on admission applications in order to obtain a place for their child at a popular school.

Sexual or physical abuse of pupils, whether by members of staff or by parents or carers, is a criminal offence and thus disclosure of such abuse is potentially covered by PIDA 1998. Sexual abuse is a problem more associated with residential schools, and children in special schools who have special educational needs are particularly vulnerable. Department for Education and Employment (henceforward DfEE) Circulars recommend that all schools and colleges should have procedures for handling suspected cases of abuse of pupils or students, including procedures to be followed if a member of staff is accused.[6] Circular 14/99 recommends that the procedures should reflect those of the Area Child Protection Committee. For example, 'Where abuse is suspected, pupils who have difficulties in communicating should be given the chance to express themselves to a member of staff with appropriate communication skills.'[7] Staff will be protected by PIDA 1998 if they disclose information from such a child, so long as they have a reasonable belief that the information tends to show that a criminal offence has been committed.

On receipt of a certificate of conviction the Secretary of State for Education and Employment is obliged to terminate the employment or direct that a teacher or youth worker should not be employed where that individual has committed certain criminal offences. This duty arises where the teacher or youth worker has been found guilty of sexual offences, such as rape or indecent assault involving a child under the age of 16. The government has recently introduced a Sexual Offences (Amendment) Bill which will make it a criminal offence punishable by imprisonment for a teacher to have a relationship with a pupil over the age of 16. Currently, a teacher whose sexual relationship with a pupil aged 16 or over becomes known to their employer is likely to be fairly dismissed. Normally, convictions leading to a sentence of no more than 30 months' imprisonment become 'spent' after a period of time ranging from 5 to 10 years.[8] This means that a person need not reveal the conviction for employment purposes and may sue anyone who maliciously reveals the conviction. However, people applying to teach are exempt from these provisions and are required to disclose all criminal convictions.

Thus PIDA 1998 will protect teachers who disclose to their employer that, for example, a member of staff or a parent has committed a criminal offence. Often the difficulty for the teacher will be determining from the information available whether a criminal offence has been committed. For example, whether or not under-age pupils have engaged in sexual intercourse. This is also related to the thorny issue of whether a teacher is committing a criminal offence when advising under-age pupils on methods of contraception. The issue of the teacher's good faith in disclosing the information is central in these situations.

Financial irregularities
Devolved school budgets have extended the concept of LMS (local management of schools). The governing body and the head teacher of a maintained school have the power to spend the annual budget for any purposes of the school. Where financial mismanagement occurs a variety of criminal offences may have been committed. However, the whistleblower may be perceived as a trouble-maker rather than as a public-spirited individual. In one case a deputy head of school was 'sacked after collecting evidence that caretakers were making false overtime claims'.[9] She successfully complained to the Secretary of State about the composition

of the governor's disciplinary panel and obtained a ruling that she had been unlawfully dismissed and was awarded compensation. She would now also be protected by the provisions of the PIDA 1998.

School admissions

The DfEE has recommended that parents who give false addresses in order to obtain a place at popular state schools should be prosecuted for fraud. An example of fraud is where parents use the addresses of relatives or friends, or rent accommodation close to the school and claim to live there. Teachers and other school staff who are aware of such a ruse are likely to be protected by the PIDA 1998 if they disclose the true position to their employer or other responsible person.

FAILURE TO COMPLY WITH ANY LEGAL OBLIGATION

'Any legal obligation' is likely to include any statutory duties as well as obligations imposed by the laws of contract and tort. The employment of teachers is regulated to a great extent by statutory provisions. Some of these measures require the head, senior teachers and other teachers to consult and communicate with each other, the LEA or the governing body. For example, a head teacher is expected to consult with the LEA and the governing body, as well as ensuring that teachers at the school receive the information they need in order to carry out their professional duties effectively. The head is also responsible for ensuring that all staff in the school have access to advice and training appropriate to their needs in accordance with the policies of the maintaining authority or governing body. Other teachers are, for example, required to make records of and reports on the personal and social needs of pupils; communicate and consult with the parents of pupil; and communicate and cooperate with persons or bodies outside the school.

Under the School Standards and Framework Act 1998 (henceforward SSFA 1998)and the LEA Code of Practice on LEA–School Relations 1999, an LEA has

1 the power to make written representations to a selection panel where the LEA considers that the panel is shortlisting an unsuitable candidate,[10] and

2 the duty to make a written report to the chair of the governing body where the LEA has a serious concern about the performance of the headteacher[11]

These provisions apply where the candidate or headteacher would have or has had a significantly detrimental effect on the performance, management or conduct of the school.[12] The Code of Practice does not specifically address the issue of 'whistleblowing'.However,it indicates the types of concern which should trigger action by an LEA and, by implication, these may be regarded examples of 'a failure to comply with a legal obligation'. Situations identified by the Code are where:

– there has been a pattern of repeated and serious complaints, over a period of time from parents, staff, governors or pupils at the candidate's previous school or schools – not all stemming from the same individual or group, but from a number of people who were originally acting in isolation from each other – which have not been satisfactorily addressed through action to investigate what substance there may be to the complaints and rectify valid causes of complaint
– the LEA of the candidate's previous school or schools suspended the school's delegated budget for reasons of mismanagement attributable to the candidate, and the school had not successfully appealed to the Secretary of State against the suspension of delegation
– there is significant evidence of continuing and systematic weakness in the management of the school or in its financial controls which, if not tackled, risks significant disruption to the school's continuing operation

These provisions support the argument that failure to deal effectively with complaints and mismanagement of the school's budget amount to a breach of a headteacher's contract of employment. Thus PIDA 1998 might protect workers who raise concerns or make disclosures of this nature.

The Secretary of State also has the power to suspend or regulate a person's employment on medical grounds; on grounds of misconduct; or, in the case of a teacher,on educational grounds. Details of all barred persons together with the kind of employment they may undertake, if any, are held in 'List 99' which is kept by the DfEE.[13] PIDA 1998 might protect a teacher who discloses such information relating to a fellow member of staff, so long as the concern is raised with their employer or the Secretary of State and the information supplied tends to show a failure to comply with a legal obligation. In any case, employers of a teacher or youth worker who is dismissed or resigned on grounds of misconduct are under a duty to report the facts of the case to the Secretary of State.[14] The misconduct arrangements also apply to both teaching and non-teaching staff employed in non-maintained special schools.[15]

FURTHER AND HIGHER EDUCATION

That whistleblowing is as important in further and higher education as it is in schools can be demonstrated by a number of examples. These include the dispute over academic standards at University College, Swansea and the allegations of financial irregularity at the University of Portsmouth. An appropriate starting point for a discussion of whistleblowing in these sectors is to refer to three recommendations contained in the Second Report of the Nolan Committee:[16]

> Recommendation 7. 'Institutions of higher and further education should make it clear that the institution permits staff to speak freely and without being subject to disciplinary sanctions or victimisation about academic standards and related matters, provided they do so lawfully, without malice, and in the public interest.'
>
> Recommendation 8. 'Where it is absolutely necessary to include confidentiality clauses in service and severance contracts, they should expressly remind staff that legitimate concerns about malpractice may be raised with the appropriate authority (the funding council, National Audit Office, Visitor or independent review body, as applicable) if this is done in the public interest.'
>
> Recommendation 10. 'The higher education funding councils, institutions and representative bodies should consult on a system of independent review of disputes. A similar process of consultation should be undertaken by the equivalent further education bodies.'

Recommendation 7 clearly reflects the Nolan Committee's view that freedom of speech is 'an important check on impropriety'. Recommendation 10 aims to ensure that concerns are properly considered and investigated and, if necessary, independently reviewed. In addition to focussing on matters which would constitute 'qualifying disclosures' under PIDA 1998 (see chapter 2), the Nolan Committee also raised issues specific to further and higher education, such as threats to academic freedom.

The further education sector is subject to a high degree of external scrutiny from a variety of bodies, including the Department for Education and Employment, the Further Education Funding Council's Audit Service and Inspectorate, the National Audit Office and colleges' own auditors. However,the existence of such external controls should not excuse colleges or their managers from actively trying to prevent wrongdoing. Following the circulation of a *Model Code of Ethics for Colleges* in December 1997,the Association of Colleges published a revised guidance note entitled *Adopting A College Procedure On Whistleblowing* in June 1998. The introduction to this document recognizes that 'there is a balance to be struck between the right of the individual to speak freely on a range of matters and the right of a college or colleagues to protect themselves against false and malicious accusations'. It also emphasizes that a whistleblowing procedure 'is not meant to be another mechanism for employees to raise private grievances'.

While acknowledging that a model procedure would be too prescriptive, the document nevertheless offers 'Good Practice Guidelines'. These are adapted from a checklist prepared by the charity Public Concern at Work, which was recommended by both the Nolan Committee and the Audit Commission. Colleges are encouraged to create a climate of openness by:

SETTING THE CONTEXT

- involving employees,listening to their concerns
- establishing a common understanding of 'right' and 'wrong'
- endorsing Codes of Practice, for example Codes of Conduct for Corporation Members and employees which define the appropriate and acceptable standards of behaviour
- ensuring openness by having a Register of Members' Interests which are routinely updated and open to public inspection

- explaining the definition of corruption, fraud and malpractice and its effect on public services
- having a policy to combat fraud in accordance with good corporate governance
- make it clear that the college is committed to the fight against fraud, corruption and malpractice whether the perpetrators are internal or external to the college
- ensure that the college procedure on whistleblowing is included in a staff handbook and issued to the employee on the commencement of employment
- if corruption, fraud or malpractice is discovered, deal with it seriously and urgently. If employees are not confident that the college will deal with the problem, they will be reluctant to raise the problem
- the Board, college management and employees should know which practices are unacceptable (for example gifts, hospitality etc.). This should be incorporated into an employee code of conduct
- encourage the unions to endorse and support this approach.

BE OPEN TO CONCERNS

- it is never easy for employees to report concerns, especially where there may turn out to be fraud, corruption or malpractice
- try to ensure that management is open to such concerns *before* they become part of a grievance or other action and do not let management's lack of action become part of the grievance
- ensure the college supports concerned employees and protects them from reprisals. Do everything possible to guarantee confidentiality
- ensure that internal audit systems and procedures minimize opportunities for fraud, corruption or malpractice to occur
- aside from line management, provide other routes to raise concerns within the organization if appropriate, for example the clerk/secretary to the Corporation, the audit committee, etc.

DEALING WITH CONCERNS

- remember there are two sides to every story
- respect and heed legitimate concerns about the employee's own safety or career

- emphasize to management and staff that victimizing employees or deterring them from raising a concern about fraud or corruption is a serious disciplinary offence
- make it clear that abusing this process by maliciously raising unfounded allegations is a serious disciplinary offence and in the case of making such an allegation externally, this would involve the offence of bringing the college into disrepute
- make it clear that legitimate concerns should be raised if they are in the interests of the college, staff, students or the public and that they should not be raised merely for the purpose of furthering any private dispute
- ensure that the college reports back to the concerned employee the outcome of the investigation and the action that is proposed'[17]

In developing a local procedure it is suggested that colleges should consult with the recognized trade unions and consider the following matters:

1 a separate procedure for whistleblowing or the adaptation of existing college procedures?
2 what should the procedure cover?
3 respecting confidentiality
4 who should be responsible for investigating the allegation?
5 timescales
6 access to the governing body
7 access to external bodies
8 malicious accusations
9 training

(It should be noted that most of these issues are discussed in chapter 5 where the possible contents of whistleblowing procedures is examined.)

In September 1999 the Committee of Vice-Chancellors and Principals of the Universities of the UK (henceforward CVCP) circulated a report entitled *Public Interest Disclosure Complaints in Higher Education Institutions.* The word 'complaint' is used in the report to mean 'an allegation or disclosure within an institution in those areas identified in the Nolan Report, which include academic freedom, and those additional areas that now fall within the scope of the Public Interest Disclosure Act 1998'. Because a 'complaint' may be made by any person, the report covers students and members of governing bodies as well as staff.

The report sees no reason why internal procedures for dealing with whistleblowing should be uniform across higher education. Nevertheless, it is recommended that such procedures should contain the following features:

1 the Registrar/Secretary/Clerk to the Governing Body should be the designated Officer to whom the complaints are addressed in the first instance
2 the internal procedure for investigating complaints should be fair, effective and robust,and a written record should be maintained at every stage of the investigation
3 the person conducting the investigation should not be the person who will have to take decisions based on the investigation
4 the identity of the complainant should be kept confidential, if so requested, for as long as possible, provided that was compatible with proper investigation
5 anonymous complaints may be reported, investigated or acted upon, but regard should be taken of the seriousness of the issue raised, the credibility of the complaint, the prospects of being able to investigate the matter, and fairness to any individual mentioned in the complaint
6 a complaint made in good faith, which was not confirmed by subsequent investigation, should not lead to any action against the complainant; but a complaint made maliciously, vexatiously or persistently which was not confirmed by subsequent investigation,could lead to disciplinary action against the complainant.[18]

Having discussed the principle of independent review and the possible role of Visitors, Ombudspersons and panels of independent persons, the CVCP recommends that institutions should ensure that their whistleblowing procedures have an independent review mechanism. It is also suggested that 'universities should ensure that any non-university institutions of higher education,or further education institutions, which they validate,accredit or otherwise recognise formally, have adequate internal procedures for dealing with staff and student complaints, as well as a public interest/whistleblowing procedure with an independent mechanism. In these circumstances, universities should also ensure that their own procedures permit them to investigate or rule on matters arising in the partner institution where appropriate'.[19]

According to the CVCP, a whistleblowing procedure should cover the following matters:

- commission of a criminal offence
- failure to observe a legal obligation,or to comply with the instrument of governance
- miscarriage of justice
- endangered health or safety or the environment
- financial or non-financial administration and malpractice
- obstruction or frustration of academic freedom
- academic or professional malpractice
- improper conduct or unethical behaviour
- suppression or concealment of any information relating to any of the above

The CVCP propose that the Audit Committee should be empowered to investigate a complaint and ensure that internal procedures are properly applied. However, it also suggests that a separate body is established to deal with 'complaints of a non-financial nature, and called the Public Interest Disclosure Committee'. Another feature of the CVCP's document is that when all internal procedures have been exhausted 'the complainant' may ask for the matter to be referred for independent review. The person(s) conducting such a review would have the power to make the following binding recommendations: (i) ordering a further internal investigation; (ii) ordering the university to re-consider the findings of the investigation. In addition,there would be power to make non-binding observations relating to the substantive complaint. Another interesting feature is that the independent person could decide, in appropriate cases, 'whether the complainant should be required to make a contribution to the costs incurred in external review'. The circumstances contemplated are where the complainant was actuated by some improper motive or the complaint was without substance or merit.

In its advice on whistleblowing, the National Association of

Teachers in Further and Higher Education (henceforward NATFHE) outlines what union branches should be looking for when scrutinizing draft procedures.[20] Included in the checklist of general points to bear in mind is the statement that 'once a proper procedure is in place there is an obligation to use it'. However, in relation to external disputes machinery, NATFHE believes 'it should be up to the individual whistleblower to choose whether to refer an unresolved problem to such machinery or to decide that another appropriate body – such as the Funding Council or the National Audit Office,is the correct one'. (See chapter 2 on the protection afforded to workers who refer their concerns to persons prescribed under PIDA 1998.)

Not surprisingly, NATFHE advocates that recognized trade unions should be involved in the process of drawing up procedures and emphasizes the importance of giving workers the option of disclosing information to a union adviser. However, since union representatives have no special rights in relation to disclosures (see chapter 2 on the position of legal advisers), it should be made clear to members that information passed to their representatives 'cannot be subject to any confidentiality requirement that puts the union representative in breach of any legal obligation'. On the confidentiality of the investigation process, NATFHE recommends that 'any allegation concerning individuals should be told to them, together with supporting evidence, so that they have an opportunity to comment'. (See chapter 9 for a discussion about union representation for both the discloser and the subject of an allegation.) Finally, on the general issue of openness, NATFHE comments that formal whistleblowing procedures should be used to value the contribution that workers can make to challenging malpractice and should not be used to 'stifle the open discussion of difficulties within institutions'.

CONCLUSION

The issue of whistleblowing has tended to be associated with different concerns in schools to those raised in further and higher education institutions. However, with their greater financial independence, schools may benefit from examining the procedures adopted in colleges and universities which have experienced such independence for a decade. Similarly, further and higher education institutions need to move on from the traditional issue of safeguarding academic freedom and give more thought to the way in which concerns about staff–student relationships might be handled.

NOTES

1. Employment Rights Act 1996, Section 43C(2).
2. LGMB *Confidential Reporting Code*, London, 1998, paragraph 5.1.
3. NUT *Whistleblowing or Public Interest Disclosure*, Circular 88/99, London, 1999.
4. NASUWT *Whistleblowing Policy Guidelines*, London, 1999.
5. See chapter 2.
6. DfEE *Protecting Children from Abuse: The Role of the Education Service*, DfEE Circular 10/95, London, 1995.
7. DfEE, *Non-Maintained Special Schools*, Circular 14/99, London, 1999, paragraph 15.
8. Rehabilitation of Offenders Act 1974.
9. An unreported case involving Jenni Watson and the Sydney Smith School in Hull. See: *The Times Educational Supplement*, 14 February 1997.
10. SSFA 1998, Schedule 16, paragraph 16(4), Schedule 17, paragraphs 17(4) and 30(3).
11. SSFA 1998, Schedule 16, paragraph 23, Schedule 17 paragraph 22.
12. LEA, *Code of Practice on LEA–School Relations*, 1999, paragraphs 111(a), 113(a).
13. DfEE, *Misconduct of Teachers and Workers With Children and Young Persons,* Circular 11/95, London, 1995. There is no statutory basis for such a list, although one will be supplied by the Protection of Children Act 1999 when it is brought into force.
14. Education Teachers, Regulations 1993, SI 1993/543, paragraph 11.
15. DfEE, *Non-maintained special schools*, Circular 14/99, paragraphs 33,34.
16. *Second Report of the Committee on Standards in Public Life*: 'Local Spending Bodies', London, HMSO, CM 3270, 1996.
17. Association of Colleges, *Adopting A College Procedure on Whistleblowing*, London, 1998, pp. 4–6.
18. Committee of Vice-Chancellors and Principals, *Public Interest Disclosure Complaints in Higher Education Institutions*, London, 1999, paragraph 12.
19. Committee of Vice-Chancellors and Principals, *Public Interest Disclosure Complaints in Higher Education Institutions*, London, 1999, paragraph 36.
20. NATFHE, *Whistleblowing*, London, 1999.

9

A Trade Union Perspective on Whistleblowing

JENNIFER FRIEZE AND KAREN JENNINGS

INTRODUCTION

The Public Interest Disclosure Act 1998 (PIDA 1998) is very important to workers because fear and intimidation still exist at some workplaces. PIDA 1998 heralds the end of 'gagging clauses' and, we hope, regimes where staff who want to work hard and contribute to high standards are criticized and blamed for poor management and practices which are a risk to health and safety. Trade unionists want to see a more open culture, where whistleblowers are seen as a safety net and not as trouble-makers – a culture which recognizes the valuable role workers can play in alerting employers to problems and making our society safer, more efficient and accountable, and free from corruption.

In this chapter we look at the background to PIDA 1998, drawing on experiences in the health service. Most of the high-profile whistleblowing cases in the public services took place in the health sector when it was being reorganized in the 1990s. These cases brought public attention to the problems staff faced speaking out against wrongdoing, malpractice and health and safety risks. We then go on to explain:

- what the new legislation means for trade unions
- the importance of whistleblowing policies and procedures
- the advice we give to negotiators
- the benefits to union organization of developing good practice around whistleblowing, and
- some of the difficulties with the legislation

BACKGROUND

The market-style health service reforms under the NHS and Community Care Act 1990, which created self-governing trusts, a new management ethos and new lines of accountability, led to mounting secrecy, intimidation and ethical dilemmas being faced by many staff. The reforms also brought about intensified workloads, the extension of roles and duties, and job insecurity, all of which contributed to increased violence and stress at the workplace. In this environment many staff had serious concerns about declining standards of care and working conditions. With the insertion of 'gagging clauses' into employment contracts, the atmosphere in the health service deteriorated and many staff became anxious and resentful about their professionalism being compromised by commercial interests. There was a steady stream of high-profile media cases involving NHS workers who suffered because they had raised concerns in the public interest.

One of the most damaging legacies of this time was that staff were often too frightened to speak up and, when they did, they were labelled as trouble-makers, disloyal or naïve, and unable to cope. Many were victimized by being disciplined or dismissed from their employment. Professional staff who were bound by codes of conduct were caught in a dilemma. They faced potential punishment by their employer for speaking up or being disciplined by their professional body for breaching a code of conduct which obliges them to speak up if they are concerned about standards of care. Along with other trade unions in the sector, UNISON campaigned for the removal of 'gagging clauses' and for legal protection for those who suffered because they raised concerns. The sympathetic response our campaign received from the press and public forced many trusts to remove explicit 'gagging clauses' from employment contracts. However, in many cases, unwritten rules continued to deter staff from raising concerns. With the election of the Labour Government in 1997, Ministers moved quickly to restore trust among NHS staff. In September 1997, the Minister for Health announced an end to 'gagging clauses' and the intimidation of staff. The government also gave full backing to the Private Member's Bill on Public Interest Disclosure.

WHAT PIDA 1998 MEANS FOR TRADE UNIONS

Workers are often in the best position to know when the public's interest is being put at risk. Staff can act as an early warning system on safety issues and help uncover fraud and mismanagement in the workplace. Unfortunately, workers contemplating 'blowing the whistle' on wrongdoing often fear they won't be listened to or that they will be putting their jobs at risk. The legal protection offered to workers under PIDA 1998 is a very important step in encouraging staff to raise concerns.

Unions have a major role to play in creating an open culture at the workplace, in raising concerns with management and ensuring that policies and practices are fair and have the confidence of staff. They can also help change the culture by making members realize that speaking up about concerns is important. Unions provide support for members who 'blow the whistle' and have established a role as watchdogs. Branch officers and shop stewards have a key part to play in raising concerns about wrongdoing and in assisting members to speak out. With the new legislation, there is a need to negotiate agreements which both help to protect whistleblowers and ensure that their concerns are taken up.

The Nolan Committee on Standards in Public Life[1] highlighted the importance of employers having effective whistleblowing policies. These could help develop a culture of openness within an organization and enable employers to find out when something is wrong in time to take the necessary corrective action. PIDA 1998 does not require employers to adopt whistleblowing policies but it gives them an incentive to do so. Unless there are effective procedures in place which demonstrate an organization's willingness to listen to and address concerns, workers are more likely to make external disclosures and be legally protected in doing so (see chapter 2). An effective whistleblowing policy can also help foster good relations, avoid crisis management and minimize damaging incidents and unpleasant publicity.

Not surprisingly, an increasing number of organizations in both the public and private sectors are introducing whistleblowing procedures (see chapter 5). In our view, whistleblowing arrangements are particularly important where organizations are providing services for the public. A survey of post-1992 universities and higher education colleges conducted by the National Association of Teachers in Further and Higher Education in September 1999 found that 56 per cent had whistleblowing procedures in place and a further 33 per cent had draft procedures. However, only about half of those with agreed or draft procedures made provision for external disclosure when internal avenues proved unsatisfactory.

Many trade unions have issued advice to branches on PIDA 1998, with detailed guidance being offered on the main provisions to include in whistleblowing policies.[2] Most of the advice that unions have circulated to their branches is similar, though some provide additional service-specific guidance where it is appropriate to their sector. For the purposes of this chapter, we will use the UNISON guidance as the basis for illustrating the type of advice unions are providing. Before looking in more detail at UNISON's recommendations to negotiators, it is worth highlighting the importance unions attach to employers providing all workers with training about their whistleblowing procedures. We also believe it is vital that mechanisms are established to monitor and evaluate how effectively concerns are being dealt with under employers' whistleblowing procedures.

WHISTLEBLOWING POLICIES AND PROCEDURES

Management style and workplace culture have a significant impact on staff health. A major cause of stress at work and work-related ill-health is lack of control and lack of participation in the decision-making process. Trade unions have a vital role to play in setting the agenda for change through collective bargaining. Whistleblowing policies and procedures are crucial to the smooth running of an organization. They form part of a range of inclusive employment policies that will enable an open culture to develop. They also allow the free flow of information and recognize the importance of strong internal communications between employers and staff. By way of contrast, a 'cover-up' culture relies on control and creates a climate of repression, fear, intimidation and disloyalty.

Our experience has shown that members who have blown the whistle have a high level of integrity and are established in their career and domestic lives. In many cases the effects of whistleblowing have led to enormous personal suffering. Not only have whistleblowers been victimized at work but in many cases they have lost their job, social standing and income, with consequential knock-on effects to their personal and family lives. Trade unions have a responsibility to seek ways to prevent such suffering and to ensure safe standards of conduct and the delivery of high-quality services. Negotiating an agreed policy and procedure on whistleblowing will help to protect employees from such victimization.

It is important that trade union representatives place whistleblowing policies on the agenda of negotiating committees, as a first step towards introducing whistleblowing codes and procedures. UNISON has provided its branches with a negotiators' guide to whistleblowing, called *Speaking Out Without Fear*. This guide outlines a comprehensive whistleblowing policy and procedure for representatives to use as a model in negotiations with their employers. It is essential that employers are made fully aware of the benefits to be gained from implementing such a policy. Trade union representatives need to argue that a whistleblowing policy would place a mutual duty on the employer and employees to resolve areas of concern internally, unless there are exceptionally serious circumstances. It is also vital that negotiated agreements acknowledge and endorse the role of the trade union. The policy should explicitly state that employees may seek advice and representation from their union representatives. This is particularly important to union members, who are able to gain access to free legal advice via their branch or regional office. Members will need to consult with a representative who has knowledge of PIDA 1998 and an understanding of the agreed policy and procedures.

ADVICE TO NEGOTIATORS

UNISON's guide was developed to help branch representatives negotiate policies and procedures that would provide maximum legal protection for whistleblowers and ensure their concerns were taken up. It gives advice on how to deal with a range of cases, including members who choose to act independently, those who blow the whistle before seeking advice, dealing with whistleblowing cases in branches and conflicts of interest.

A WHISTLEBLOWING POLICY AND PROCEDURE FOR THE WORKPLACE

Speaking Out Without Fear explains to branch representatives that whistleblowing agreements provide important protection for workers wanting to raise concerns about wrongdoing or malpractice. It also emphasizes that branch representatives have a key role to play in raising concerns about wrongdoing and in assisting members to speak out. In drafting the guide, we considered recommending anonymous whistleblowing, i.e the member would disclose information to a union representative, who would in turn raise the concern on behalf of the union but conceal the member's identity. However, there were several arguments against this arrangement.

First, protection for workers who raise concerns anonymously is difficult to invoke under PIDA 1998. If an employer suspected the worker's identity and victimized or dismissed them, it could be difficult to prove that whistleblowing was the reason for the unfavourable treatment. Second, PIDA 1998 only protects individual workers who raise concerns and gives no special status to union representatives. Thus union representatives have to take the same steps as any other worker to ensure that a concern is raised in ways protected by PIDA 1998 (see chapter 2). For these reasons, we recommend that negotiators ensure that whistleblowing agreements allow them to advise and represent members wanting to raise concerns. This would enable union representatives to raise concerns with their employer on behalf of members. We recognize there may be cases where, after the concern was investigated, the employer will ask the whistleblower(s) to identify themselves and give evidence. Nevertheless, we advise union representatives to keep all disclosures confidential and that agreements ensure confidentiality for the whistleblower if this is requested.

ADVICE FOR MEMBERS CONCERNED ABOUT MALPRACTICE

In most situations where malpractice is suspected, workers should be able to raise their concerns with their line manager without fear of reprisal. If members are anxious about raising their concern in the workplace,they may choose to consult with their union representative. Members may be afraid that their colleagues or manager will turn on them or they may be worried about the damage that could be caused by a disclosure about serious malpractice or corruption. Thus we suggest that representatives make sure they identify *why* members are seeking advice. Branch representatives are urged to treat all cases sensitively.

It is very important that the whistleblower has a reasonable belief that the wrongdoing or malpractice has occurred. Therefore we advise representatives that, if possible, members should try to get supporting evidence from colleagues to corroborate their concerns, especially before making a disclosure to a 'prescribed person' (see chapter 2). In the vast majority of cases where there are whistleblowing policies and procedures at workplaces, concerns can be dealt with internally. Representatives are advised to ensure that members follow the procedures and raise their concerns internally, either with their line manager or a designated officer who acts as an alternative point of contact. Similarly, representatives are urged to ensure that employers are given the opportunity to investigate and respond to concerns that have been raised. Where a whistleblowing policy provides that trade union representatives can advise and represent members, such representatives can raise concerns on behalf of members with the appropriate line manager or designated officer. Again, representatives are advised to check that there are reasonable grounds to suspect wrongdoing.

In serious circumstances or where members fear victimization, a cover up or a life-threatening situation, disclosures can be made externally. Where such action is contemplated, we urge representatives to ensure that members get legal advice and assistance through their union. Members must also be made aware that disclosures are only protected under PIDA 1998 if they are made in good faith. Representatives will also need to advise members that an initial interview with the appropriate line manager or designated officer will be required. At this stage, a brief report would be written, which should be agreed by both parties. It would then be shown to the most senior person in the organization, who would set up a further investigation if appropriate. Representatives should aim to negotiate agreements which specify that workers will be given regular feedback on the outcome of any investigation. Time limits should be allocated for each stage of the procedure. If the time limits pass without satisfactory action being taken, the agreements should provide for the concerns to be raised at the next level. If whistleblowers are not satisfied with the outcome of the investigation, they may be justified in making an external disclosure. Representatives have an important role to play in advising members whether or not this is a reasonable course of action.

ADVICE FOR MEMBERS WHO CHOOSE TO ACT INDEPENDENTLY

Sometimes members may choose to act independently. This may be because they do not agree with the advice they have been given by their branch representative or it may be because they feel strongly about the issue and want to be associated with it. Whatever the reason, we advise representatives to make the member aware of possible problems and pitfalls. We also ask representatives to ensure that the member is aware of the workplace policy and procedure and any professional codes of conduct governing standards of practice.

It almost goes without saying that the member should be encouraged to think about the consequences of whistleblowing. For example, is the member alone or supported by colleagues, and do colleagues have the same sense of resolve as him or her? Members should be encouraged to examine their motives and try to identify who is suffering. Equally, they should assess what toll the stress might take on their personal life and career and whether they have the determination to see it through. After considering all this, if the member still wishes to act independently, it will be recommended that they: ensure that they are familiar with the whistleblowing policy and how to use it; gather evidence and information that will support the alleged wrongdoing; stick to the facts and avoid personal arguments. Members will also be informed that they can contact Public Concern at Work, the specialist charity working in this field,for further advice.

CASES WHERE A MEMBER BLOWS THE WHISTLE BEFORE GETTING ADVICE

Branch representatives may have to deal with cases where a member has 'blown the whistle' externally to the media before seeking advice from the trade union. Depending on the prominence given by the press, the member may need a lot of emotional support. The member should also be informed about any whistleblowing policy and procedure, the protection provided under PIDA 1998 and the desirability of obtaining legal advice through the union. In such cases, representatives are encouraged to try to protect the member and to assess how to limit the effect of any damage from the disclosures. It is recommended that representatives call a meeting to decide how to support the member. For example, members may decide to mount a campaign for changes in the workplace to remove the original cause for concern. We also suggest that representatives consider developing a strategy with other trade unions who may be affected.

CONCERNS ABOUT BRANCH REPRESENTATIVES

UNISON has set up procedures for dealing with cases where members have concerns about branch representatives at their workplace. Where a member has a concern about the work of a branch representative, they have the right to take it to the regional or national office. Branches have been asked to ensure that members are aware that they can get advice from their regional office or from the national office under these circumstances. Of course the union has to be satisfied that the matter is not simply a complaint about the level of service provided by the branch or a regional official. Where a concern about a branch representative is genuinely raised in the public interest, the regional office will advise the member how to follow any whistleblowing procedure at the workplace. However, if the member's concern is about the response of trade union representatives to an industrial relations difficulty, the matter will be dealt with under the union's complaints procedure.

CONFLICTS OF INTEREST

Where the whistleblower and the alleged wrongdoer are both members of the same branch, special arrangements are required to guarantee that both are properly represented. This is not an unusual situation for a branch to face and there are procedures for representatives to follow. Alleged wrongdoers are entitled to proper representation to ensure that any investigation conducted under the whistleblowing procedure, and any disciplinary procedures that may follow, are conducted fairly. If the concerns prove ill-founded, it will be clear to everyone how important it was that the alleged wrongdoer was represented. In arranging representation, it is recommended that the same officer should not represent both the whistleblower and the alleged wrongdoer. Branches can get assistance from the regional office in such cases but they are advised to make sure the whistleblower is not represented by an officer of lower rank than the person representing the alleged wrongdoer.

OPPORTUNITIES FOR BUILDING UNION ORGANIZATION

UNISON is providing education and training to help branch representatives understand PIDA 1998, to enable them to negotiate effective agreements and to provide advice and support for members. The union is developing structures at national and regional level to enable it to provide appropriate support for branches. Each region has appointed at least one regional officer who will provide specialist advice and act as a resource for the region. These specialist officers have been given training to assist them to carry out their role more effectively. Branches and officers are being encouraged to negotiate whistleblowing policies and procedures with employers. A database of agreements is being set up and branches are being asked to ensure their policies and agreements are held on the database. Agreements will be monitored and examples of good practice will be shared across the union.

UNISON is streamlining arrangements for providing legal advice in whistleblowing cases to ensure that there is consistency of treatment for members. The union is also establishing systems to monitor and evaluate how whistleblowing cases are dealt with. Public Concern at Work helped prepare UNISON's guide to branches and has assisted with its training programme. It also provides expert advice to members, branches and officers through its advice line. The union itself offers advice through its national Whistleblowers 'Hotline'. Recognizing that whistleblowing is never going to be easy, this 'hotline' was established to offer reassurance and a listening ear. Members are referred to the most appropriate union representative closest to their workplace for further assistance and access to specialist advice. This will usually be provided by their branch representative. All calls are treated in strict confidence.

UNISON's strategy on whistleblowing has been carefully planned and is being coordinated across the union. It believes that PIDA 1998 provides opportunities for working in partnership with employers to change the culture at the workplace. It also offers important opportunities for branches to build up their organization and involve members in forging a new workplace culture. UNISON believes unions can provide the best protection for whistleblowers and regards establishing good whistleblowing policies and agreements as an important tool for recruitment.

POSSIBLE DIFFICULTIES WITH THE LEGISLATION

Because of the way PIDA 1998 has been framed, there are a few areas which could cause problems for trade unions.

INDIVIDUAL VERSUS CLASS ACTIONS

There is no specific provision enabling a group of workers, or a representative acting on their behalf, to raise a concern. Where a whistleblowing policy and procedure so provides, a union representative can raise concerns on behalf of an individual worker or a group of workers. However, the protection provided by PIDA 1998 only applies to workers as individuals. From a union perspective, it would be preferable for this protection to apply to members of a group of workers as a collective entity. This would make it less onerous to mount legal challenges against any detriment suffered by members of the group. More importantly, it would also make the act of whistleblowing less isolating and make it easier for people to raise concerns.

HEALTH STUDENTS

Because health students, such as nursing students on pre-registration education and training courses, are classified as 'students', even when they are training and working within NHS hospital trusts, it seems that they are not covered by PIDA 1998 (see chapter 2 on the definition of a 'worker' for these purposes). This could discourage health students from raising concerns when they are working in the NHS. Since students may need to ask questions and raise concerns about practice as part of their training, this gap in the protection offered to whistleblowers could undermine the positive steps being taken in the NHS to make the culture more open. However, because the Department of Health has made it clear that all staff working in the NHS should be protected under PIDA 1998, UNISON believes it unlikely that the Department would sit idly by while a trust victimized any students who raised concerns in good faith. UNISON is advising representatives to raise this issue in negotiations on whistleblowing policies.

TRADE UNION REPRESENTATIVES AND PROTECTED DISCLOSURES

Disclosures made by whistleblowers to their union representatives are protected when the trade union is specified in the employers' whistleblowing procedure. Similarly, where a member makes a disclosure in the course of obtaining legal advice, the disclosure to the union's lawyer will be protected whether or not the union is recognized at the workplace (see chapter 2). In principle, there could be a problem if the union is not recognized at the workplace and the employee is victimized for raising a concern with the union. However, the government argues that an employment tribunal would be likely to judge the disclosure to the union to have been reasonable under the circumstances, particularly where there is no whistleblowing policy or procedure at the workplace.

The debate about whether or not disclosures to union officials should be protected is linked to the issue of confidentiality. Lawyers are bound by a duty of confidence to their clients, but trade union officials are not. The government argues that, if disclosures to trade union officials were specifically protected under the PIDA 1998, this would impose obligations of confidence on trade union representatives. The consequence of this would be that information from a member wanting to 'blow the whistle' could only be used for the purposes that were agreed by that member and not in general negotiations with the employer. For example, if the information related to a safety risk but the whistleblower decided not to pursue the matter, the union would be unable take it up with the employer even though the well-being of some of its members might be affected. The government also argues that Section 10 of the Employment Relations Act 1999 provides workers with the right to union representation and assistance during grievance and disciplinary procedures and that it is implicit in this procedure that there is a disclosure between the employee and the union representative. The government has also made it clear that it expects the word 'grievance' to cover disclosures of malpractice.

On balance, UNISON has been persuaded by the government's arguments. If employers establish suitable policies and procedures, then we believe whistleblowers will be more likely to gain proper protection under the PIDA 1998. In addition, tribunals will be more likely to accept disclosures to union representatives as reasonable. UNISON has a code of conduct and procedures which all union representatives are expected to follow. These require union representatives to act in good faith and respect confidentiality. If representatives do not follow our code of conduct, then their behaviour will be investigated and dealt with under the union's complaints procedure. UNISON will be closely monitoring employers' policies, procedures and practices, together with employment tribunal decisions. If problems arise because disclosures to unions are not specifically protected under PIDA 1998, then we will make representations to the Department of Trade and Industry.

TRADE UNIONS AS 'PRESCRIBED PERSONS'

Trade unions have not been designated as 'prescribed persons' under PIDA 1998. The Schedule of 'prescribed persons' to whom disclosures can be made includes bodies with a specific role in regulating and investigating wrongdoing, such as the Health and Safety Executive and the Financial Services Authority (see chapter 2). Trade unions have a major role to play in creating a more open culture at the workplace, in raising concerns with management and ensuring that employers' policies and practices are fair and have the confidence of staff. They also have a vital role to play in providing support for employees who 'blow the whistle'. These activities would be compromised if unions were designated as 'prescribed persons' and had an obligation to investigate wrongdoing.

CONCLUSION

PIDA 1998 is a groundbreaking piece of legislation with the potential to begin to transform relationships at the workplace by creating a more open culture. Hopefully, people wanting to 'blow the whistle' will no longer be seen as troublemakers and the potential contribution workers can make to the provision of high-quality services and the protection of the public interest will be recognized.

NOTES

1. *Second Report of the Committee on Standards in Public Life*, London, 1996.
2. Apart from our own organization, UNISON, the unions contacted were the GMB, MSF (Manufacturing Science Finance), NATFHE (the National Association of Teachers in Further and Higher Education), the National Union of Teachers (NUT) and the TGWU (Transport and General Workers Union).

10

A Whistleblower's Perspective

KATE SCHRODER

INTRODUCTION

My personal experience of whistleblowing began in 1996, just as the expression was beginning to become familiar in the tabloid press. In the same year Don Touhig's whistleblower protection measure was rejected by the House of Commons but the charity Public Concern at Work was getting to grips with a campaign which was to lead eventually to the enactment of the Public Interest Disclosure Act 1998 (henceforward PIDA 1998). My case was referred to during political debates and questions were asked in the House of Commons regarding the details of the reported wrongdoing. Few whistleblowers gain such notoriety. However, the knowledge and support of others offered only a limited comfort during the events which followed.

My research involved an investigation into the experiences of other whistleblowers, with the objective of identifying appropriate forms of support. Athough the case studies are drawn from a variety of occupational backgrounds, industrial sectors and levels within organizations, common threads emerge. Further research is necessary to ensure that both the differences and similarities between experiences are properly analysed. Empirical research using 'real whistleblowers' is uncommon and the investigation of groups of employees who have taken a decision *not* to report their concerns is even more difficult to undertake. This is because of the logistical difficulties in identifying workers who have decided not to report perceived wrongdoing or who have remained outside any of the support systems currently available to potential whistleblowers. By describing several 'real' experiences it is hoped that useful lessons may be learned about the ways in which an attempt to report serious concerns through the channels suggested by the PIDA 1998 might go drastically wrong and why a decision may be taken to 'turn a blind eye'.

To some extent the experiences of whistleblowers prior to the implementation of the PIDA 1998 might be considered by some to be the 'ghosts of whistleblowing past'. Nevertheless, they should not be forgotten entirely. Case studies indicate that reprisals may be suffered even when following the reporting routes suggested by the PIDA 1998. Indeed, it seems highly probable that this legislation alone will not be enough to protect against victimization in the future. An in-depth analysis of previous and current experience may aid the understanding of why legal protection was necessary in the UK and where gaps lie within current sources of support. It is suggested that additional forms of support, both legal and otherwise, are required so that the potential for victimization is reduced and controlled. In the writer's opinion, bona fide whistleblowing needs to be encouraged as a means of reducing risks to workers, employers and the general public.

SOME WHISTLEBLOWERS' EXPERIENCES

While some respondents described experiencing a certain amount of general unease prior to discovering specific wrongdoing in the workplace, which continued throughout their attempts to report, others said that they were unprepared either for their discovery or for the events which followed. Irrespective of the different circumstances leading up to the discovery of malpractice, similarities exist throughout the series of events which follow a decision to report. It is here that the lessons necessary to the careful and proper handling of employee concerns may be learned. Even where a person chooses not to report, it would appear that the decision-making processes do not cease but continue through the re-assessment of risk and the continued evaluation of the types of wrongdoing discovered. It follows that once malpractice is identified, the worker assumes the role of potential whistleblower. It is difficult to determine when this role might end – a decision to report may be taken after the worker has obtained new employment and no longer has contact with the alleged wrongdoer. Indeed, it is hardly surprising that respondents felt the need to reduce the risk of victimization by obtaining another job before raising the alarm. One whistleblower indicated that he wanted to distance himself from the wrongdoing but had a crisis of conscience which forced him to report to the police. Employers who dismiss potential or actual whistleblowers, or who encourage the voluntary take-up of an alternative employment, do not necessarily halt the processes of whistleblowing but simply lose control of them. Similarly, employers who choose not to provide adequate mechanisms for reporting concerns miss out on the opportunity to reduce wastage and fail to appreciate that allegations of organizational wrongdoing are best managed internally (see chapter 5).

Whistleblowers can be categorized into two main groups. Firstly, rather than looking for irregularities, many whistleblowers appear to have been taken by surprise by the discovery of malpractice. This group flies in the face of some whistleblowing theories because they did not seek out wrongdoing as part of their duties. Instead, they came upon it simply because they were in a position to observe it. Often such people are forced to make a faster assessment of information (and any associated risk) prior to reporting than the 'watchdog or lookout' group. This second group are 'primed' to locate and report wrongdoing (see below).

KAREN'S CASE

Karen had enjoyed a successful career working with adults suffering from mental health difficulties. She had experienced no concerns regarding her role or interaction with either staff or patients prior to observing the calculated abuse of one adult by a doctor during the provision of electro-shock therapy. The treatment caused the patient distress and was wrongly administered because the doctor appeared to be unfamiliar with the equipment. Karen objected to an instruction to continue treating the fully conscious patient and was told to submit paperwork which would indicate that successful treatment had been carried out. She informed a more senior nursing manager because it became evident that the doctor intended to make another attempt to administer electro-shock therapy to the same patient, who would have required a degree of constraint.

The treatment ceased but the doctor complained about Karen's refusal to follow his instructions. He offered no explanation of the events which had led up to the alleged misconduct on Karen's part. She was suspended on the basis of this allegation of misconduct, even though she had made a full report to the senior nursing manager, and a disciplinary hearing was arranged to take place within several weeks. In the meantime, she was unable to discuss the events with staff other than her union representative. The hearing found that she was without fault, mainly because the union representative knew about another nurse who had had a similar experience with the same doctor but had decided against reporting. The doctor was not reprimanded. However, Karen was forced to seek alternative employment because she found it impossible to gain promotion or to discuss her experience with other staff who had not understood the details of the suspension or hearing. While both remained upon her file and in the memories of other staff, she was unable to respond to adverse comments regarding her character, judgement or competence.

Karen explained that her decision to report the doctor was a natural reaction to the distress of the patient and that she would always protect patients in such circumstances. However, she felt dismayed that she could not expect the support of line management if she observed serious wrongdoing in the future. Karen did not have any contact with external agencies about her experience nor did she make a disclosure to the media. She rejected the idea that she was a whistleblower, insisting her actions were in response to her duty and responsibility to the patient and to her profession (see chapter 6). It is worth noting that Karen would have been protected by the PIDA 1998 (had it been in force) in relation to the victimization in her employment. However, the legislation does not assist those who are applying for alternative posts because discrimination at the hiring stage is outside its remit.

Karen still fears that she might fall foul of confidentiality and loyalty clauses and is not persuaded that recent changes to NHS contracts have altered the culture or attitudes within the sector very significantly. During her disciplinary hearing it emerged that the other nurse who had witnessed the mistreatment of patients undergoing electro-shock therapy had decided against reporting because he was fearful about contravening confidentiality clauses in his employment contract. In the face of the account given by the doctor, Karen felt that she would not have been able to withstand the pressures of the hearing had the evidence of the other nurse not supported her. In any event, the doctor had suffered no detriment to his career while Karen may be subjected to future boycotting and has been unable to shake off the stigma (perceived or otherwise) associated with her experience.

BEN'S CASE

Ben's case demonstrates how tensions relating to the duty of confidentiality exist in other professions and how retaliation may be more subtle. During the House of Commons Standing Committee debate on the PIDA 1998 it was stated that the Home Affairs Select Committee supported the principle of protecting police officers in line with the Act. Ben's experience questions whether this will be enough or if further protective measures are needed which are tailored to the particular circumstances .of policing. There are dilemmas for police whistleblowers which may not be present in other sectors, based on notions of confidentiality and loyalty, the need to speak out and to protect information sources. Although there are indications that senior officers believe whistleblowing to be an important and valid method of removing corruption, it is not felt within all of the ranks that this is either acceptable or risk-free. Some officers appear to have confused whistleblowing with entrapment and few forces have support mechanisms in place which reduce the fears of potential whistleblowers.

Ben had some concerns about the behaviour of several officers, some at the same level as himself and at least one more senior. He did not consider his conversation with me to be in contravention of his contract or any other codes relating to loyalty since it was clearly understood that his identity would remain confidential. Ben's decision not to report was based upon his assessment of personal risk. He had been in the police force for over fifteen years and thought himself unlikely to gain any other type of employment. His social life was arranged around his role within the force and contact with his peers. His partner's friends were the partners of other officers. He did not feel confident that systems were in place which would effectively provide anonymity within his social group or confidentiality in his work environment. He explained that 'like other sectors, corruption and other types of wrongdoing exist within all levels of the organization'. I asked him how he might react if there was a risk of being tainted by the wrongdoing of others. He thought such a scenario was unlikely as it was possible to ascertain the activities of others (something which is not possible in many occupations). Ben spoke about the pressures within the force to 'be one of the lads' and thought that these related to the need to support fellow officers even where the ethics of doing so became problematic.

Ben would not have been protected by the PIDA 1998 as the police have not yet been brought within the scope of the legislation. However, it is unlikely that he would have been encouraged to report even if PIDA 1998 did apply because his assessment was that the risks were greater than any potential benefits. It is also worth noting that Ben did not feel that his role as a police officer included the obligation to act as 'watchdog' for acts of wrongdoing committed by others within the profession. It seems likely that his concerns remain unreported because a culture existed of 'turning a blind eye'.

ROWENA'S CASE

Rowena was an accountant with experience of credit control in the public sector. She had worked within the NHS for fifteen years and was about to be dismissed from her job at one of the larger London hospitals when I first made contact with her. Rowena had been transferred to a new department and given the task of increasing the money returned through credit control practices. She looked at existing procedures, drew up an action plan, and presented it to her new line manager. Although the plan was agreed in principle, Rowena was unable to obtain any of the resources necessary for its implementation. During the next eight months Rowena raised her concerns about falling income levels and the use of old procedures which she knew to be unlawful. She became alarmed when she overheard her line manager and a union representative discussing her dismissal. However, when she was asked to attend a discliplinary hearing, she was not allowed to have somebody to accompany her. Rowena was dismissed for failing to meet targets. However, following an appeal, she was redeployed into a different department under the same line management. She suffered seven months of isolation and was unable to obtain independent support from her union representative, who appeared to be an associate of the line manager. Rowena was made redundant while on sick leave and is currently unemployed. She would have been protected by the PIDA 1998 because her concerns included unlawful acts, not merely maladministration (see chapter 2).

The second group of whistleblowers ('watchdogs' or 'look-outs'), includes workers who have responsibility for setting and maintaining standards. Such people understood that they should raise the alarm when necessary and became confused by an adverse reaction to their reporting through internal or external channels. Most interviewees thought that their role as 'look-out' was, in effect, being denied by the employer. Confusingly, this was the case even where the worker believed that 'watchdog' role had been encouraged. Indeed, the failure by employers to provide adequate reporting procedures suggests that the people charged with maintaining standards were not in fact expected to raise their concerns.

ROGER'S CASE

A good example of an employee primed to raise the alarm is Roger, who was head of the contracts branch for a US naval ship-yard. He was meticulous in his approach to his work, which relied upon accuracy and the close weighing of contractual obligations and safety requirements. Indeed, the lives of others depended upon his competence and attention to detail. Roger explained that previously he had experienced no qualms about his role and he was described by others as being a quiet, pleasant but fastidious man. On discovering that contracts were being awarded to ex-navy personnel and that shipyards were being closed unnecessarily, he raised his concerns through internal channels. When his memos were intercepted and an internal investigation was rejected, he appealed through external routes, including the chief of naval operations and several Senators. It was admitted that contracts had been awarded in ways which were inconsistent with good practice.

However, Roger has been unable to regain his former post, his reputation or confidence in the systems he had previously supported. He is quite open about his experience, the administrative, media and governmental routes he has followed in his pursuit of justice, and has established a web site. He understands and accepts the label of whistleblower and is associated with an informal support network. Roger feels unable to bring legal proceedings because the amounts of money involved are less than those necessary to excite interest from the specialist lawyers working on a *pro bono* basis. However, he is grateful that he was not subjected to a personal attack in response to his actions. Roger would have been protected by the PIDA 1998 had it applied in his case.

CAPTAIN FRIEND'S CASE

Being employed as a safety inspector of helicopters, Captain Friend was also primed to raise the alarm. Although he identified a number of serious concerns about the risks being faced by both pilots and their passengers, he was sacked for insisting that his concerns be heard. His initial action for defamation against the Civil Aviation Authority was quashed on the grounds that 'an employee who accepts a disciplinary code as part of his contract of employment consents to the republication of the accusation or complaint as part of that process'.[1] Thus Captain Friend could not bring an action for defamation on the republication, even if the accusations were false or malicious. Captain Friend feels that he has been denied natural justice. He secured an employment tribunal decision that he was unfairly dismissed yet was denied compensation on the grounds of contributory fault. He was also defamed during the disciplinary process but, owing to what he perceives as a legal technicality, he was denied a remedy. Captain Friend might well have been protected by PIDA 1998 had it been in force.

Many other whistleblowers have explained the fear that they might be forced to defend an action for defamation where an external disclosure is made. However, few expected that they might have to consider bringing one. Only three interviewees brought an action for defamation. Others explained that it is expensive (being operated by specialist legal practitioners), falls outside the scope of the legal aid system,[2] and places a heavy burden of proof upon the claimant. Indeed, whistleblowers frequently complain that they are denied access to the information they would need to begin legal actions of any kind, including defamation.

KATE'S CASE

My experience began when I felt that standards within my organization were lower than those experienced elsewhere or expected by external agencies. When I reported my concerns to senior managers, I was asked to make recommendations regarding the raising of standards and the attainment of targets. I made written reports to the highest level within the organization, which included specific findings of contractual non-compliance (of an increasingly serious nature) and indicated the preventative steps that I had taken. When further and more serious wrongdoing emerged, I requested instructions and made it clear that I could not act unethically or illegally. When it became clear that malpractice was continuing and independent legal advice suggested that a cover-up was under way, I reported externally to the agency appointed by the government as contract-manager (and which was also funding it). At that time the agency did not initiate an independent investigation but gave details of my identity and concerns to the employer. I was dismissed for the gross misconduct of breaching my duty of confidentiality by reporting that fraud had taken place.

I followed the reporting routes subsequently suggested by the PIDA 1998 mainly through a desire for caution and self-preservation. I contacted Public Concern at Work (henceforward PCAW) because they were mentioned in a newspaper article about people experiencing similar difficulties (see chapter 11). PCAW looked at the documents I held, including the reports and memos I had sent and received and those associated with the disciplinary hearings of other staff. It was suggested that I speak to a professional journalist who might stimulate an independent investigation. This journalist interviewed a number of people and a story was printed in the *Evening Standard*. It had been heavily edited after legal advice and a number of discrepancies appeared which were repeated by several other media outlets. These included a press statement issued by my employer which inferred that I had been dismissed for being involved in fraud and for losing the trust of the external agency. The Director of PCAW, Guy Dehn, intervened on my behalf and insisted that a further article in the *Evening Standard* was withdrawn. The journalist wrote to apologize for the way in which the stories had been presented, complaining of editorial intervention and difficulties connected to advertising revenue considerations. Other national newspapers printed interviews with me which had not taken place. An undertaking not to allow anyone to look at the documentation was forced upon me by my employer, under the threat that I would be sued for damaging their commercial activities.

Several weeks after the press articles appeared I was contacted by the fraud squad and one officer invited me to 'spill the beans'. I gave the fraud squad a copy of the notice of appeal that I had sent to my employer along with copies of relevant documents. These demonstrated that the irregularities went back to a time prior to my period of employment and that I had discovered and reported internally before being dismissed. Following my introduction to a sympathetic lawyer, an action for libel was brought against my previous employer, which was underwritten by the Sir James Goldsmith Foundation. During these proceedings it became clear that the initial piece in the *Evening Standard* had used words which did not exist on the tape or transcript of the interview with the employer.

Like many other whistleblowers, I made the decision to report malpractice internally because I felt that the organization would respond positively to my findings, which were supported by specific evidence. It was my understanding that the responsibility for any subsequent action was theirs and not mine. I made an inventory of the wrongdoing and the potential for damage to the organization, because that was within my prescribed remit, and asked the immediate line manager for instructions. No whistleblowing procedure existed. Receiving no response, I took specific details and supporting documentary evidence to the highest level of management. Only as a last resort was a disclosure made to the proper external agency. When professional and legal advice indicated that a cover-up was taking place, I made a media disclosure which led to police inquiries. The Serious Fraud Office took over the investigation during 1998 and my libel action continued until I received a satisfactory settlement in January 1999. Although I would have been protected by the PIDA 1998 had it been in force, I would not have been able to complain about boycotting by prospective employers because, as mentioned earlier, discrimination at the point of hiring is not regulated by this Act.

CONCLUSIONS AND RECOMMENDATIONS

In the light of experience and my research findings, I would make the following recommendations:

1 Seek sound specialist and/or legal support from someone willing to keep the concerns confidential. Where union advice is

sought, take care to ensure that information will not leak back to an unintended person and that a report will not be made without permission being sought and given. At least one case study has shown that the identity of a potential whistleblower and her concerns were given to an alleged wrongdoer by a union representative. It should also be borne in mind that, unless an employer's reporting procedure indicates that the union is an appropriate recipient of concerns, any disclosure made to them may not be protected by PIDA 1998 (see chapter 9).

2 Once a decision to report internally is made, care should be taken to ensure that existing reporting procedures are followed, unless it can be shown that a cover-up may ensue or that victimization would follow. Where reporting procedures are not in place, it may be wise to approach the most appropriate highly placed person within the organization. Where file notes are made or copies of documentation taken, it should be understood that this may be a breach of an employee's contract, especially where confidential information is disclosed externally.

3 Where it proves necessary to make a report to the police, or an interview is arranged, it is recommended that another person who is familiar with the circumstances attends and that notes of the meeting are taken. I believe that the negative role of 'informer' should be rejected. The word 'informer' was thought by most respondents to describe wrongdoers turned evidence-providers, whereas whistleblowers were thought to be innocent and concerned witnesses or bystanders. During the course of my research it has emerged that many police officers failed to distinguish between whistleblowers and informers.

4 Where contact with the media is absolutely necessary, care should be taken about who is approached and the amount of control others are given in relation to the publication of material. The use of a legal advisor at this stage appears to make some difference and may offer protection against pressure to give further interviews. Anyone making a media disclosure should also be aware that the organization about which concerns are raised will respond and that an action for defamation might need to be brought or defended.

5 Most respondents stated that they had experienced feelings of

helplessness at some stage of the whistleblowing process. This resulted from a lack of feedback, isolation during the investigation into the concerns raised and a rejection of the idea that they were at any stage being proactive. Most said that they merely responded to others and did not fully accept the view that they had a power to influence the series of events which took place during or following reporting. In my opinion, workers must understand the responsibility that accompanies any decision to report or to ignore serious wrongdoing and the ways in which their behaviour might influence the actions of others, positively or otherwise.

6 Most respondents did not use whistleblowing procedures, stating either that none were in place or that they were not whistleblowing. In two cases employers did have specialist reporting procedures. One was not made fully available to all employees while the other was apparently in operation without the knowledge of the particular individual. In my opinion, all employers should have whistleblowing procedures and communicate them to all staff. They should be reviewed regularly and included at induction and appropriate further training events. Workers need to be familiar with the reporting procedure and participate in both its design and evaluation, if possible.

7 Lastly, employers can help to reduce negative perceptions of whistleblowing within their organizations by identifying what they regard as serious wrongdoing. Equally, it should be clearly stated when other mechanisms should be utilized, for example grievance or equal opportunities procedures.

It goes without saying that it is far better to minimize the opportunity for wrongdoing than to seek to prevent whistleblowing. A culture of openness and the application of policies and procedures to all levels of the organization should help to reduce the risk of wrongdoing. Hopefully, one effect of the PIDA 1998 will be that appropriate reporting procedures will become widespread. If so, many of the adverse reactions to whistleblowing will diminish. Until such time, it would be wise to remember the reasoning behind PIDA 1998 – why it was thought necessary and why it gained such overwhelming support.

NOTES

1. See: *Friend v Civil Aviation Authority [1998] IRLR 253.*
2. Note now the possibility of actions being brought on a 'no win, no fee' basis.

11
Providing Advice on Whistleblowing
CHIDI KING

INTRODUCTION

History is littered with unfortunate tales of whistleblowers. Employers commonly regarded such people as troublemakers; disloyal workers who bit the hand that fed them. More often than not, those who found the moral courage to speak up against malpractice in the workplace would find themselves at best isolated, usually out of a job and sometimes out of a career. Society in general viewed the whistleblower as no better than a sneak or a turncoat.

Jim Smith and Stanley Adams are just two examples. Smith, a director of a UK defence company, discovered evidence of overpricing on some of the company's contracts with the Ministry of Defence. He insisted that this was rectified and that the company repay the excess of around £1 million. The company refused and, for his honesty, Smith was instantly dismissed. Smith notified the MoD of his concerns, which eventually led to the MoD recovering more than £1 million in overpaid profits. Although his actions were praised by the Public Accounts Committee,[1] Smith found himself penniless, homeless and with his career in ruins. The case of Stanley Adams is even more tragic. Adams exposed the price-fixing activities of the multinational drug company Hoffman La Roche to the European Commission. The company was fined £150,000 and forced to alter its practices. Adams, however, was arrested by the Swiss authorities for industrial espionage – his disclosure was in breach of Swiss secrecy laws – and given a one-year suspended jail sentence. While he was in prison awaiting trial, his wife committed suicide.

More recently, the experience of Paul van Buitenen, the European Commission internal auditor who blew the whistle on fraud and corruption, will do little to encourage other conscientious workers to follow in his footsteps. Although his disclosures to the European Parliament forced the resignation of the entire college of Commissioners, and his actions were largely vindicated by an Independent Committee of Experts, Mr van Buitenen was suspended, disciplined and demoted.

A series of catastrophic yet preventable scandals and disasters in the 1980s alerted the public (and ultimately the legislature) to the importance of whistleblowers. Time and again the inquests into these events revealed that, although workers were aware of the malpractice, no one had dared to blow the whistle. Alternatively, where someone had found the courage to speak up, the concerns had fallen on deaf ears.

When the UK suffered one of its most serious rail disasters in 1988, with the loss of 35 lives, the public inquiry found that a supervisor had noticed the dangerous wiring that led to the crash. He had said nothing because he did not want to rock the boat. The inquiry into the sinking of the *Herald of Free Enterprise* at Zeebrugge in 1987 found that staff had warned on no less than five occasions that the ferries were sailing with the bow doors open. 193 passengers lost their lives.

In 1993 four children failed to return home after setting out on a canoeing trip with an outdoors activity centre. Several months before these children drowned, two instructors had sent a letter to the managing director of the centre warning him that safety measures needed to be drastically improved if just such a tragedy were to be prevented. The warning was ignored. However, the existence of the letter led to the UK's first successful prosecution for corporate manslaughter.

The fall-out from these incidents was, needless to say, devastating for the families who lost loved ones, for the workers and investors who lost livelihoods and for the companies themselves. However, these events were not only damaging for those directly involved. They also rocked public confidence in the ability of UK institutions to self-regulate and protect the interests of the ordinary person.

PUBLIC CONCERN AT WORK'S EXPERIENCE

BACKGROUND

It was in this climate that the independent charity Public Concern at Work (PCAW) was launched in 1993. The founding director,

Guy Dehn, was the legal officer at the National Consumer Council. His responsibilities had included drafting the Council's response to some of the public inquiries mentioned above. The founding trustees of the charity included Lord Borrie QC, Professor Ross Cranston (now the Solicitor General), Maurice Frankel (Director of the Campaign for Freedom of Information) and Marlene Winfield (of the National Consumer Council). The founders of PCAW noted the common link in the findings of the public inquiries and took the view that, if employee concerns being voiced and heeded could have prevented these disasters, then the same had to be true for lesser incidents of corporate negligence or misconduct. While not on a scale to merit a public inquiry, such incidents could nevertheless have shattering consequences for those involved.

As part of its broader brief 'to promote ethical standards of conduct and compliance with the law' by organizations in all sectors, a key activity of the charity would be to provide sound legal and practical advice to workers with concerns about serious malpractice. An independent national helpline was set up and staffed by qualified lawyers, enabling employees to obtain direct confidential advice about their public concerns free of charge. Provided that such concerns were raised in the right manner and were properly acted on, then this would reduce the likelihood of major disasters in the future,[2] would help to promote better corporate governance and would increase the accountability of organizations.

With the prevailing tendency of employers to shoot the messenger, scant legal protection for whistleblowers and no readily identifiable independent, confidential and accessible source of advice, little wonder that workers would rather turn a blind eye to malpractice. Despite what may now seem the obvious benefits of a working environment where staff can speak up in safety, when PCAW was first set up few were persuaded of the need for an organization to provide advice – much less legal advice – to whistleblowers. Nonetheless, in the first year of its launch, with relatively little publicity, PCAW received over 380 calls to its helpline from workers with serious concerns ranging from financial malpractice to abuse in care. The need for the service was clearly established.

RESEARCH

If further proof were needed of the value of whistleblowing in maintaining standards and probity, research undertaken by PCAW[3] in the first three years of its existence provided just that. PCAW's study into malpractice in the police force – a culture where a premium is placed on loyalty to colleagues – revealed that, far from speaking up against instances of serious malpractice, the tendency was for officers to support corrupt colleagues to the extent of giving false evidence in court. Such confused loyalty had cost the police force dearly in terms of public perception and confidence and in monetary terms.[4] Where officers did speak up, they were systematically squeezed out of the force. For example, one officer was prosecuted (and acquitted) for perverting the course of justice after refusing to lie about an incident he had witnessed. The officer had witnessed a senior officer kick and stamp on the face of a suspect. He was then ordered by a sergeant to lie about the incident. When he reported the matter to his divisional head, he was charged with perverting the course of justice. The officers who were involved in the assault on the suspect were later tried and convicted. Commenting on attempts by senior officers to cover up the incident, the trial judge said, 'You were acting on false loyalty. It would have been better for everyone if you had been prepared to protest.'

PCAW's research into financial malpractice in the defence sector reveals further the perils of speaking up in organizations whose culture is imbued with a misplaced sense of loyalty and priorities. In one case, a Ministry of Defence (MoD) official, with some reluctance, blew the whistle on a colleague who was running up huge expense claims. His claims were investigated and the colleague was suspended pending a disciplinary hearing. Several weeks later the official was entertaining a journalist to a working lunch. He made a claim for £9.60 for sandwiches and two pints of beer consumed at the lunch during which they had been joined by several colleagues and civilians. The official was subsequently arrested for defrauding the MoD. It was alleged that one of the pints of beer bought at the lunch was not consumed by the journalist as claimed on the expenses form but by someone who had joined them. He was suspended pending disciplinary action. It took seven and a half months for the disciplinary case to be resolved, after which the MoD official was cleared of the charges. However, he was not allowed to return to his former job. He was told that the vacancy no longer existed and was given new duties in a small office which was also used as a changing room. The revised duties also meant that his salary was much reduced. A strange 'reward' for someone who had acted to prevent his employer being defrauded and to protect the public purse.

WORKING WITH EMPLOYERS

Providing advice and support to whistleblowers would ultimately prove to be a futile exercise if the culture in organizations remains non-conducive to speaking up. PCAW works closely with employers to develop working environments where staff are encouraged to come forward with their concerns, with the assurance that those concerns will be properly investigated and that the worker will suffer no adverse repercussions. There has been a gradual shift towards such openness, helped considerably by the Nolan Committee's[5] recommendation that all public bodies should adopt whistleblowing procedures. Increasing numbers of employers in the public, private and voluntary sector are adopting and implementing whistleblowing procedures (see chapter 5). However, by and large employers still need to be persuaded that whistleblowing can have more positive than negative effects. No one wants to hear bad news. Yet surely it must be better to hear such news from the mouth of a loyal and conscientious member of staff than from a customer, a regulator or the media?

THE HELPLINE

Public Concern at Work was not the first organization to provide advice and support to whistleblowers. For example, trade unions have played a vital role in this area (see chapter 9). However, PCAW was the first in the UK to provide concerned employees with direct access to specialist legal advice, especially in those organizations where there was no union representation. Typically, callers to the helpline feel isolated, uncertain about whom to talk to, unsure whether their concern is wholly justified and fearful that speaking up will only create more problems by upsetting the status quo. Statistics from the helpline show that there is no unique profile of a whistleblower. Concerned employees come from all walks of life, occupy all levels of position and can be found in any sector (see chapter 10).

In its first five years, PCAW has provided advice and assistance to over 1,300 whistleblowers. 46 per cent of callers to the helpline worked in the private sector, 44 per cent in the public sector and 10 per cent in the voluntary sector. As a rule, a whistleblower is most likely to be a junior employee concerned with the activities of his or her more senior colleagues. However, PCAW has advised senior hospital consultants, trustees of charitable organizations and senior managers as well as nurses, carers and manual workers. In 1995, for example, 4 per cent of clients occupied executive positions, 13 per cent were in management, 15 per cent belonged to a profession, 31 per cent were skilled, 29 per cent were unskilled and 8 per cent held administrative posts. As to the concerns themselves, over the five-year period 36 per cent related to financial malpractice, 21 per cent to workplace safety, 15 per cent to public safety and 14 per cent to abuse in care.

The way in which the whistle is blown can help to determine whether the employer shoots the messenger or listens to the message and whether the worker keeps their job or becomes another newspaper 'hard luck' story. Accordingly, the advice PCAW gives focuses on the practical aspects of whistleblowing, without losing sight of the worker's legal position. The advice given takes account of the risks and opportunities of raising concerns and seeks to ensure that the concern is raised in a responsible and constructive way rather than in an aggressive or confrontational manner. The earlier the whistleblower is able to seek advice, the less likely it is that things will go badly wrong. The charity receives a large number of calls from whistleblowers who complain of experiencing victimization at the hands of their employers as a result of raising concerns about malpractice. Commonly, at this stage both employee and employer have adopted entrenched positions and the original concern has escalated into a grievance about the treatment of the employee.

THE PRACTICALITIES OF WHISTLEBLOWING

The following checklist contains some helpful tips for potential whistleblowers.

WHISTLEBLOWING CHECKLIST

To speak or not to speak?
This can be a difficult decision because most whistleblowing concerns will involve an allegation of wrongdoing by an individual or group of individuals. While you should not be expected to prove that your concern is well founded, you should be able to show that there are good reasons for your suspicions.

- Writing things down can help to focus and clarify matters in your own mind. Keep a record of the events that have led to your suspicions.
- Seek confidential advice at the earliest opportunity, from your trade union, professional organization, Public Concern at Work or other advice agency.

Raising the concern
In most cases it will be best to raise the concern internally. After all, your employer is best placed to investigate and correct any malpractice. Going outside the organization without first giving your employer the opportunity to put things right will elicit a defensive response and is more likely to make you the focus of unwelcome attention. Additionally, internal disclosures are more readily protected by the Public Interest Disclosure Act 1998 (henceforward PIDA 1998) (see chapter 2).

- Resist the temptation to blow the whistle anonymously. This would make your concern more difficult to investigate and does not guarantee that others won't deduce who blew the whistle. If you are victimized and seek to bring a PIDA 1998 claim, you will face the added hurdle of proving that your employer knew that you blew the whistle.
- If your employer has a whistleblowing policy and procedure, use it. If not, try to identify someone senior within the organization who you feel confident will listen to your concerns and has the authority to take matters forward.
- If others share your concerns, try to enlist their support in coming forward: a collective voice is stronger than a single voice. If you belong to a trade union, their support will be invaluable.

- Keep a sense of perspective. It is for your employer to investigate the concern and decide what action, if any, should be taken. You may not always agree with your employer's decision. For example, you may think that the perpetrator of the malpractice should be sacked. Your employer may decide that a lesser sanction is appropriate. The important thing is that the malpractice is stopped, that measures are put in place to prevent recurrences and that those in charge can account for their decisions.

There may circumstances where you feel that that you have no choice but to go outside the organization, as the case studies below demonstrate. This may be because you work for a small employer and/or the malpractice goes to the top of the organization, because urgency and/or the seriousness of the malpractice demands it, or because your internal disclosures have been ignored.

- Again, seek advice about your legal position as soon as possible.
- Remember that PIDA 1998 provides valuable guidance on how outside disclosures should be made.
- Make sure that you have gathered together some good evidence to support your concerns.
- Choose the person to whom your disclosure will be made with care. Appropriate disclosures to a regulator or the police, for example, may be more effective and far less damaging for all concerned than a disclosure to the media.
- Be realistic about the likely consequences of your disclosure to yourself, your colleagues and the organization.

SOME CASES FROM THE FILES OF PCAW

The three cases which follow illustrate the dilemma faced by whistleblowers and the importance of easy access to advice and support.

SEXUAL ABUSE IN A RESIDENTIAL HOME

Judy was employed as a deputy matron in a private nursing home for the elderly run by Mr and Mrs T. Some of the residents were blind and some suffered from senile dementia. Mr T was a very well respected member of his local community with a long career in the care sector and had received an award from the Archbishop of York for his services to the community. Judy had misgivings about Mr T for some time. Things came to a head one afternoon when a care assistant told her that she had entered one of the resident's rooms and found Mr T behaving strangely next to one of the female residents. When the care assistant returned to the room with Judy, Mr T had left. However, they found what appeared to be semen on the resident's cardigan and in her hair. Judy's first concern was for the resident and she swiftly cleaned her up and washed the cardigan, incidentally disposing of any evidence.

A few weeks later, Judy heard of Public Concern at Work and contacted us. She did not know where to turn. If she confronted Mr T he would simply deny that anything untoward had happened and would probably then find a reason to dismiss her. Without the evidence to support her suspicions that Mr T had forced oral sex on the resident, she felt unable to approach the police as it would be her word against his. We advised Judy to keep a vigilant eye on Mr T and to try to ensure that he was not left alone with any of the female residents. If another incident occurred, we asked Judy to take care to preserve any evidence and to contact us immediately.

Several months later, Judy telephoned the helpline. The previous night she had entered a room where there were two blind ladies and one with senile dementia. Mr T appeared to have his groin in the face of the lady with dementia. When Mr T had left the room, Judy returned with a colleague. With a clean swab, they took a specimen from the resident's mouth. Getting the specimen analysed presented hurdles. The police could not arrange a forensic test unless there was a formal complaint. However if Judy made a complaint, the police would have to question Mr T even if the test proved negative. This put Judy in an invidious position. After much toing and froing between the police and the Social Services Inspectorate, PCAW decided to pay the costs of the test. The Forensic Laboratory collected the swab from Judy's home and within 24 hours the sample had been analysed and found to contain semen. We forwarded the evidence to the local CID who interviewed Judy and arrested Mr T the next day. At first Mr T denied the allegations, but once presented with the forensic evidence he capitulated. He pleaded guilty to three charges of indecent assault and was sentenced to jail for four years.

A CASE OF FRAUD

Adrian worked at the local site of a major waste disposal firm. He was concerned that his colleagues were defrauding a local paper mill. Adrian suspected that some employees of the mill were being paid to steal top grade paper, which was then concealed among waste paper in skips that were collected daily by a waste paper company. When the company delivered the waste to Adrian's firm, the paper was also sold on for cash at a fraction of the market cost. Adrian was reluctant to identify himself initially and was concerned that the perpetrators were influential in his firm and had good contacts with the local police. He described the atmosphere at the site as intimidatory and the managers as bullying and abusive. He feared that, if he spoke out, not only would he lose his job but his life would be made intolerable. From the information that Adrian gave us, we were satisfied that the matter should be looked into. With Adrian's agreement we contacted the victim of the apparent fraud, the local paper mill. Although the company initially suspected that we were a security company seeking new business, they soon realized that their procedures left them open to such a fraud.

Within a couple of weeks the company caught two of its staff engaged in the scam red-handed. However, they were unable to identify the size of the fraud or how long it had gone on. Having obtained assurances that Adrian would suffer no adverse repercussions, we put the company's investigators in touch with Adrian. He was able to show them how the fraud had been concealed in the paper work. With this information, the company realized that the fraud had cost it some £3 million. The police were called in and arrests were made. The boss of the waste paper company was convicted and sentenced to three years, and others involved were jailed for several months. Adrian's foreman was sacked, the charge-hand resigned and the manager of the site took early retirement. The local paper mill recovered almost £1 million from its insurers and so averted plans to close down with the loss of over one hundred jobs.

PROTECTING PUBLIC SAFETY

Ian worked as a safety inspector at an amusement park. He was responsible for maintaining one of the park's most popular rides. Every morning he would carry out a safety inspection on the ride and, if it passed, he would sign the ride off as safe in the log. During one inspection he noticed that the pins on the axles which kept the carriages stable had become loose. Ian thought this presented a serious risk and notified his managers accordingly. After what Ian felt was a cursory examination, the operations manager cleared the ride as safe. Ian was unhappy with this and, because no corrective action had been taken, he failed the ride the next day. Again, the operations manager overruled him and Ian was assigned to other rides.

Ian contacted us the same day. He was anxious that the weekend was coming up and that the park would be extremely busy. He was also worried that if he pursued the issue any further he would be dismissed. We advised Ian that we would contact the HSE on his behalf and relay the information that he had without giving his name. However, it was more than likely that they would want to speak to him if they felt that the situation was potentially serious. We said we would explain Ian's anxieties about his position and ask the HSE to bear this in mind. While he was unsure whether he would agree to speak to the HSE, he asked us to make the initial contact.

The HSE agreed that the situation sounded potentially serious. However, they told us that they would need to speak to Ian. We explained his fears that if the HSE suddenly turned up to inspect this particular ride, his employers would easily put two and two together and he would be out of a job. The HSE assured us that if they were to carry out an inspection, it could be done in such a way as not to make Ian's role apparent. We went back to Ian and, after talking things through, he agreed that he would speak to the HSE. Shortly afterwards the HSE made a 'routine' visit to the park during which they inspected the ride along with several other rides. As a result of the inspection, the ride was suspended and necessary repairs were carried out.

CONCLUSION

The term whistleblowing is losing its pejorative meaning. Increasingly employers are recognizing the role their staff can play in providing them with critical information in sufficient time to avert risks and dangers. More and more employers across all sectors are adopting whistleblowing policies. However, there is still a long way to go before whistleblowing is generally perceived, by employers and employees alike, as a safe and accepted thing to do.

The Public Interest Disclosure Act 1998 should help expedite a change in culture, much in the same way as the anti-discrimination legislation.[6] The PIDA 1998 sends a clear message to employers and to society that whistleblowers are an indispensable safety net against corporate malpractice and excesses which threaten the public interest. In the shorter term the PIDA 1998 should help counter the tendency to shoot the messenger. In the longer term the Act will help promote an open and accountable workplace culture, where speaking up is the norm rather than the exception.

NOTES

1. The UK parliamentary select committee charged with the scrutiny of public expenditure accounts.
2. It should come as no surprise that soon after the UK suffered its second worse rail disaster of recent times – the 1999 Paddington crash – it was revealed that the rail companies had resisted calls to introduce a confidential reporting procedure, i.e. a 'whistleblowing' procedure through which staff could report safety concerns without fear of recrimination.
3. Public Concern at Work, *Speaking up by Sector: The Police*, London, 1993; Public Concern at Work, *Speaking up by Sector: Local Government*, London, 1994; Public Concern at Work, *Speaking up by Sector: Defence Procurement*, London, 1995; Public Concern at Work, *The Law and Practice on Whistleblowing in Europe*, London, 1995.
4. The exposure of widespread corruption in the Stoke Newington police force and West Midlands Crime Squad, for example, did much damage to the reputation of the entire UK police force. In 1990, the Metropolitan police force paid out £139,215 in compensation in just two cases where officers were alleged to have fabricated evidence.
5. *Second Report of the Committee on Standards in Public LIfe*, London, 1996.
6. Sex Discrimination Act 1975, Race Relations Act 1976 and Disability Discrimination Act 1994.

Index